I0804277

PRAISE FOR

LIES IN DISGUISE

"*Lies in Disguise* is a perfect title for my friend Gail's book. Half-truths and distortions don't just affect the media. The same thing is happening to Christian doctrine. This book not only helps sincere Christians recognize half-truths. It also equips you to explain these lies to others."

— **Steve Saint**, son of martyred missionary Nate Saint,
Founder of ITEC mission ministry and author of
The Great Omission, *End of the Spear* and *Walking His Trail*

"In *Lies in Disguise*, Gail Purath tackles hard issues with kindness, compassion, and biblical truth. She exposes the lies and half-truths that confuse and deceive our world and counters them with well-researched reasoning and scriptural thinking. For pastors, parents, and every thoughtful Christian who wants to stand for biblical truth, this book provides everything we need to mount a solid defense."

— **Lori Hatcher**, author of
Lord, I Believe: 60 Devotions for Your Troubled Heart

"It is my pleasure to recommend Gail Purath's book. It presents clearly and concisely arguments countering errors concerning the truths of Scripture that are finding acceptance among some Christians and churches. The issues are complex, and not every true Christian will agree on every point, but this book presents the issues fairly, gives well-reasoned arguments based on Scripture, and provides follow-up questions suitable for further study and group interaction."

— **Chip McDaniel**, ThD, Professor of Old Testament and Hebrew (Ret.),
Southeastern Baptist Theological Seminary, Wake Forest, NC

"Anyone who appreciates solid apologetics will love this book! Gail is highly skilled in analyzing the culture's intentional distortions of Bible passages, correcting common misconceptions, and addressing today's "normalized" sins while helping readers understand and defend clear, biblical truth. In *Lies in Disguise*, Gail's crisp, comprehensive analysis is thoroughly sprinkled with Scriptures that not only serve as proof texts but also engage readers to pursue and examine God's truth for themselves. This is a significant, deception-busting book!"

— **Dawn Wilson**, founder and director of Heart Choices Today and blogging at TruthTalkWithDawn.com

"In a culture where lies persist and truth is hard to find, Gail Purath dispels many of the most prevalent lies that can shipwreck a believer's faith and gently leads us back to the truth about God's character and will for our lives. New believers and even many long-time believers cannot afford to ignore Gail's teaching and corrections."

— **Scott Koeman**, Chaplain (Colonel), U.S. Army

Half-Truths
Many Christians
Believe

LIES IN DISGUISE

Gail Burton
Purath

CLC
PUBLICATIONS
Fort Washington, PA 19034

Lies in Disguise: Half-Truths Many Christians Believe

Published by CLC Publications

USA: P.O. Box 1449, Fort Washington, PA 19034
www.clcpublications.com

UK: Kingsway CLC Trust
Unit 5, Glendale Avenue, Sandycroft, Flintshire, CH5 2QP
www.equippingthechurch.com

This printing 2026

For permission to reprint, please contact us at
permissions@clcpublications.com

Printed in the United States of America

ISBN (paperback): 978-1-61958-330-6
ISBN (ebook): 978-1-61958-416-7

Italics in Scripture quotations are the emphasis of the author.

*I dedicate this book to my momma, Erma Burton,
who loved God and His Word and set an example
for me even before I came to know Christ.*

CONTENTS

PREFACE

WHEN I BECAME a Christian at age 24, one thing that drew me to the Lord and excited me about my newfound faith was the fact that God had divinely inspired a book to teach us truth. I was confused about right and wrong and good and evil, and I was tired of hearing conflicting human views.

In the fifty years since I gave my life to Christ, my love and respect for God's Word has continually deepened, as has my distrust of human wisdom. "Has not God made foolish the wisdom of the world?" (1 Cor. 1:20).

In his farewell to the Ephesians, Paul warned, "I know that after I leave, savage wolves will come in among you and will not spare the flock. Even from your own number men will arise and distort the truth in order to draw away disciples after them. So be on your guard!" (Acts 20:29–31).

The body of Christ has always faced challenges identifying and rejecting worldly philosophies that slip into Christian teachings. The most effective false teachers are those who use a mixture of truth and error, combining Scripture with human wisdom. Because Christians have a high regard for Scripture, we are more apt to be taken in by these "lies in disguise." These half-truths also appeal to our fallen human desires, downplaying the serious nature of sin and redefining love as acceptance.

In the modern church, a movement called Progressive Christianity attempts to redefine Christ, salvation, and sin. Because these teachings appeal to our pride and our desire to fit in with culture—and because many people don't take the time to study the Bible for themselves—these teachings have become radically popular.

Many of those who promote these half-truths are *New York Times* bestselling authors with enormous followings. Some of my loved ones have walked away from their faith because of these false teachers, so you can understand why writing this book is important to me.

But this book is not about Progressive Christianity. I expose some of their half-truth propaganda in Chapter 15, which discusses gay revisionist theology, but the rest of the book is about the subtle half-truths that have paved the way for acceptance of more progressive errors. If you are not surprised by any of the half-truths in this book, you are an extremely rare Christian. I admit that I believed many of these "lies in disguise" before I carefully and prayerfully researched them.

As Paul explained in Acts 20, false teachers and false teachings are nothing new. They've been around since the beginning of time, as you'll discover in the Introduction, which explains the origin of the half-truth method of deception.

You'll also find a section at the end of each chapter called "Digging Deeper: Questions for Group or Personal Study." I hope you'll take time to answer these questions that further reinforce the truths in the chapter. Better yet, I encourage you to read this book with a friend or small group, discuss what you learn, and do the Digging Deeper questions together.

While I am a woman writing this book, it is not a "women's book." The truths I explore are rooted in Scripture and relevant to every believer, male or female. I have been encouraged by the fact that men as well as women read my devotional blog, *Bible Love Notes*. I've researched this topic and found broad agreement among biblical scholars that Christian men can benefit from materials written by Christian women—because authorship is not the same as exercising spiritual authority.

My husband, who is the head of our home, is also my closest friend, advisor, and champion in this writing ministry. Though he doesn't enjoy writing himself, in many ways this book is a shared effort. We both believe that writing is part of God's purpose for my life (Eph. 2:10), and we offer this book to all readers—men and women alike—who desire to know and walk in truth.

So sit back with your Bible in hand, and prepare to read the Scriptures referenced in every section of the book. Like the noble Bereans in Acts 17:11, confirm your beliefs based on God's Word.

Introduction

Why Half-Truths Are More Deceptive than Outright Lies

STUDIES SHOW that after people form an opinion, they usually refuse to listen to facts that refute it.[1] If the belief is a mixture of truth and error, it's even harder to give up. That's why including Scripture in false teachings has always been one of Satan's favorite tactics.

If we are going to live faithfully, we need to be open to correction, and we need to let go of any belief that contradicts God's Word. We must "do [our] best to present [ourselves] to God as one approved, a worker who does not need to be ashamed and who correctly handles the word of truth" (2 Tim. 2:15).

That means checking everything against the full counsel of Scripture and refusing to take things out of context. It means becoming familiar with common methods false teachers use, so we recognize truth and error and improve our discernment.

Satan Instituted the Half-Truth Method

Satan, the father of lies, invented the half-truth tactic in the garden of Eden. It worked so well that he's been using it ever since and inspiring others to use it. It involves including a little truth to give an air of validity to his lies. And when he

1 Elizabeth Kolbert, "That's What You Think," *The New Yorker*, February 27, 2017.

fully deceives people, he often gives them a false "form of godliness" even though his lies deny the power of the gospel (2 Tim. 3:1–5).

Satan's half-truth tactics are recorded throughout Scripture as warnings for us. In the garden of Eden, he told Eve that if she ate the forbidden fruit, she'd be like God, understanding good and evil (Gen. 3:4–5).

> ***Throughout Old Testament times, Satan distracted humans with half-truths about pleasure and pagan practices.***

Eve listened to Satan and found out he was half right. Eating the fruit didn't make her more like God, but she better understood good and evil because she lost her innocence and introduced sin and death into her perfect world (Gen. 3).

Throughout Old Testament times, Satan distracted humans with half-truths about pleasure and pagan practices. Instead of inheriting the blessings of the Promised Land when God planned to give it to them, the people wandered in the wilderness for another generation. And when they finally entered the land, they continually rebelled, trying to mix pagan lies with God's truth and suffering the consequences.

This happened throughout Scripture, but let me offer a few specific examples.

Kingly Half-Truth Hypocrisy

Satan inspires the use of half-truths to change the course of history and to justify disobedience. The story of King Saul's final demise in First Samuel 15 is one example. God instructed Saul to completely destroy the Amalekites and all of their possessions. Their evil ways had fully contaminated everything in their country. We don't always understand God's Old Testament commands to destroy entire nations, but we know He is perfectly good and wise, patient and long suffering, giving people and nations ample warnings. Everything He does is perfectly just.

So, Saul carried out God's explicit orders . . . sort of . . . well, not exactly. He destroyed the Amalekites, but he made the king his prisoner, and he kept the best of the livestock. When the prophet Samuel confronted him, Saul told this half-truth: "I have carried out the LORD's instructions" (1 Sam. 15:13). This is such a clear illustration that half-truths are no different than outright lies.

When Samuel pointed to the captured livestock, Saul tried to blame that decision on his men, claiming they took the animals to sacrifice to the LORD. Nothing in Scripture leads us to believe that Saul's claim was true. Instead, he was piling half-truth upon half-truth because of his half-hearted obedience. No wonder Samuel explained that Saul's rebellion was "like the sin of divination" and his arrogance "like the evil of idolatry" (15:23).

Saul insincerely apologized to spare himself embarrassment in front of his men (15:30), and even though he remained king after this fatal flaw, he lost God's approval and anointing (15:35). This story is an important warning because Saul's attitudes negatively affected his life and the nation of Israel.

The same is true for spiritual leaders who obey God half-heartedly and share half-truth teachings to make Christianity more culturally acceptable. They damage individuals as well as churches and nations.

Satan Attempts to Trick the Word Using the Word

Perhaps the most ridiculous example of Satan's half-truth methods is when he tried to tempt Jesus. He used God's Word, thinking he could confuse Jesus who *is* the Word (John 1:1–5)!

Forty days without food made Jesus hungry, and Satan did his best to take advantage of that hunger. Satan likes to tempt us when we're vulnerable: hungry, sick, tired, or preparing for ministry tasks. He tempted Christ to turn stones into bread as a proof that He was the Son of God (Matt. 4:1–11). Christ responded with Scripture: "It is written: 'Man shall not live on bread alone, but on every word that comes from the mouth of God' " (Matt. 4:4; Deut. 8:3).

Then Satan tried quoting Psalm 91:11–12 and encouraging Jesus to prove He was God by jumping from the top of the temple so angels could rescue Him. Jesus again responded by quoting Scripture: "It is also written: 'Do not put the Lord your God to the test' " (Matt. 4:7; Deut. 6:16).

Satan's final foolish request was for Jesus to worship him in exchange for all the kingdoms of the world. Jesus said, "Away from me, Satan! For it is written: 'Worship the Lord your God, and serve him only' " (Matt. 4:10; Deut. 6:13).

Nothing Satan did could confuse or mislead our Lord Jesus, but Satan has much more success with his human victims, taking them captive with half-truth human philosophies (Col. 2:8). Christ gave us an example to follow when we face half-truth teachings: When someone quotes a half-truth, we should respond with a full-truth!

Twice the Credit for Half the Truth

In the New Testament, we find the story of Ananias and his wife, Sapphira, telling what might be called an "uncharitable half-truth." God undoubtedly wanted us to understand the serious nature of their sin because He dropped them dead in their tracks. If this were the punishment for telling a half-truth today, we'd have an epidemic of dead Christians.

Acts 4:32–37 gives us the background: The Christians were sharing their assets with each other. Barnabas sold a field and gave all the money to be distributed to those in need. Then Acts 5:1–11 tells that Ananias and Sapphira sold a field and pretended to do the same thing as Barnabas—but they actually kept some money for themselves. Peter said they were under no compulsion to give the full amount to the church, but pretending they had done so was an attempt to lie to the Holy Spirit (Acts 5:3).

When they were both struck dead, "Great fear seized the whole church and all who heard about these events" (5:11). This was an appropriate kind of fear—a healthy fear of the Lord that helped these new Christians realize that they couldn't play games with God. Ananias and Sapphira were setting a deadly precedent, and God would not have it.

Half-Truth Omissions

I read a story about a man arrested for driving under the influence of caffeine. Several legitimate news sources ran the story before finding it was only half true. The man was indeed arrested and a test showed caffeine was the only substance in his blood. But he was arrested for reckless driving, not for drinking too many espressos. The blood test ruled out driving under the influence of alcohol, but it didn't blame his recklessness on caffeine.

Sadly, some things taught in the church mimic this kind of reporting. As we've seen with other examples, half-truth teachings omit certain facts and highlight others. And one example in Scripture clearly illustrates this "cut-and-paste theology." But before sharing that passage, let me give an early American example.

Thomas Jefferson didn't agree with the whole Bible, especially miracles, the resurrection, and the Holy Spirit. So he cut out those portions of Scripture and created the Jefferson Bible.[2]

I doubt he realized he was taking his cues from another political leader who lived thousands of years before him, King Jehoiakim. The Lord told Jeremiah to write a prophecy and read it to King Jehoiakim. When Jeremiah read it, the king listened to it a few lines at a time and "cut them off with a scribe's knife and threw them into the firepot, until the entire scroll was burned in the fire" (Jer. 36:23).

2 Owen Edwards, "How Thomas Jefferson Created His Own Bible," *Smithsonian Magazine*, January 2012.

Most of us don't take scissors to God's Word like Jefferson and Jehoiakim, but a growing number of Christians ignore passages or create sophisticated arguments to explain them away. They create a Jesus in their own image, emphasizing aspects of His character they like, and ignoring or denying aspects they don't like—a clear sign of false teaching.

Context Matters

Let me offer another analogy for understanding half-truth, cut-and-paste theology. Years ago, a fast-food restaurant aired commercials calling another restaurant's chicken nuggets "pieces parts" because they were made of bits and pieces of chicken pressed together. You could say the pieces of meat were "out of context" because they no longer had the texture or shape of chicken meat.

> ***False teachers are handing us "junk food" in place of the "bread of life" (John 6:35).***

In the same way, some Christian teachings have been so manipulated that they have little resemblance to the living Word of God. By cutting certain verses out of context and pressing them together, false teachers form attractive half-truths that are tasty to undiscerning Christians. You might say these false teachers are handing us "junk food" in place of the "bread of life" (John 6:35).

Modern technology allows a photographer to manipulate a picture, placing a person in a location where they've never been. The media can take a few phrases of a speech and make a politician look good or bad. Taking things out of context is an easy and effective way to mislead people.

Imagine someone quoting, "Man shall not live on bread alone" (Matt. 4:4) and saying Jesus was promoting a low-carb diet. Or suppose your child's Sunday school teacher told her class to do their best to be annoying because "Blessed are you when people insult you" (5:11).

These claims sound ridiculous, but they resemble some of the half-truths circulated in the modern church. We must remember every verse in the Bible is true, but not every verse contains complete truth. We must combine it with the immediate context, the context of the book, and the context of Scripture as a whole.

We are blessed that our God gave us a book, not a handful of verses. That's one reason Scripture commands us to "Study and be eager and do your utmost to present yourself to God approved (tested by trial), a workman who has no cause to be ashamed, correctly analyzing *and* accurately dividing [rightly handling and skillfully teaching] the Word of Truth" (2 Tim. 2:15, AMPC).

Digging Deeper: Questions for Group or Personal Study

To better understand the way half-truths confuse, sugarcoat, and misrepresent the gospel by taking things out of context, take some time to do this short study on prayer.

1. Read Matthew 7:7. If this were the only verse on prayer, what could you conclude?

2. Now read John 14:14 and 15:7, James 4:3, First John 3:21–22 and 5:14–15, and explain how each passage adds to our overall understanding of biblical prayer.

3. The passages in questions 1 and 2 help us better understand prayer, but we may still have questions about the way God answers our prayers. These passages can help us deal with our unanswered questions: Deuteronomy 29:29; First Corinthians 13:12; Isaiah 55:8–9.

4. Even though it's unlikely that Saul was telling the truth about his men taking the livestock to sacrifice to the Lord, let's suppose that was true. Is it possible to disobey God in order to honor Him? See First John 2:3–4 and Titus 1:16.

SECTION 1

The "Judge Not" Half-Truth

You may be surprised to find four chapters dedicated to an accurate understanding of biblical judgment, but the "judge not" half-truth is deeply ingrained in Christian thinking and rhetoric, and it negatively affects important commands of the gospel.

1

Understanding Matthew 7:1–5

ONE OF THE most prevalent half-truths of our time may be the "judge not" error based on Matthew 7:1. It's a popular reproof used by saved and unsaved people alike. At times, "judge not" is an appropriate rebuke. But most often it's used inappropriately. So let's start by discussing the key passage where this half-truth originates, Matthew 7:1–5:

> Do not judge, or you too will be judged. For in the same way you judge others, you will be judged, and with the measure you use, it will be measured to you. Why do you look at the speck of sawdust in your brother's eye and pay no attention to the plank in your own eye? How can you say to your brother, "Let me take the speck out of your eye," when all the time there is a plank in your own eye? You hypocrite, first take the plank out of your own eye, and then you will see clearly to remove the speck from your brother's eye.

Several years ago, my husband noticed distorted vision in one eye. A few weeks later, he had surgery to repair a macular hole. Before the surgery and during the healing process, his view of things was quite distorted. When someone has a macular hole, they can look at a piece of graph paper and instead of seeing a grid of straight lines the person will see curved, twisted, darkened, and distorted lines. This is a good example of the word picture God gives us in Matthew 7:1–5 regarding distorted spiritual vision.

"Planks," as mentioned in this passage, might be things such as unrepentant sin, bitterness, hypocrisy, pride, and selfishness which distort our spiritual view.

Without surgery, my husband might have eventually gone blind. If we don't deal with planks biblically, we'll eventually go spiritually blind. And removing our planks not only benefits us, it also equips us to help fellow believers to remove the specks and planks from their eyes.

I'm grateful that physicians could restore my husband's physical vision, and I'm grateful the Great Physician can restore our spiritual vision when we repent.

A Childish Point of View

Now let's look at how Matthew 7:1–5 became a half-truth.

Suppose a mother tells her teenaged daughter, "Don't go to the store or you'll waste your time. First check the pantry, make a list, and then go to the store prepared."

Only a young child without reasoning skills would think the mother was telling her daughter never to go shopping. Older children and adults would understand that the mother's opening sentence was only one part of the full instructions.

> ***When we study Scripture, we must be aware of the immediate context as well as the full teaching of God's Word.***

Sadly, the childish view of Matthew 7:1–5 has become more popular than the actual meaning of the passage. Instead of reading the full five verses and placing the opening phrase in context, people use that phrase to claim all judgment is inappropriate. This is especially ironic because the final verse explains that removing our planks equips us to judge the specks in others' eyes.

When we study Scripture, we must be aware of the immediate context as well as the full teaching of God's Word. Otherwise, we'll be like unreasoning children, "mere infants in Christ" (1 Cor. 3:1), believing popular half-truths.

Judging is Necessary

The "judge not" half-truth teaching has effectively silenced many Christians from sharing God's truth in appropriate ways. And it's an unrealistic expectation. It's impossible not to judge because judging nothing means believing nothing.

Recently, I read a celebrity quote that proved this point. An actress claimed she was totally nonjudgmental because she approves all the different views about sexual lifestyles and practices. She added that Christians are stupid, dangerous, and judgmental because they disagree with her.

She clearly illustrates the type of hypocritical judgment condemned in Matthew 7:1–5. Claiming to be nonjudgmental, she harshly judged Christians. Claiming to accept all points of view, she fully rejected the biblical view. She also proved the point that no one is completely nonjudgmental. Before we address biblical ways to judge, let's look at other judgmental errors besides this obvious type of hypocrisy.

Don't Emulate Job's Friends

The first chapter of the book of Job describes God's view of Job: "There is no one on earth like him; he is blameless and upright, a man who fears God and shuns evil" (Job 1:8).

When Job lost his children, wealth, and health, his friends came to "comfort" him. But instead of comforting Job, they spent many hours trying to convince him that his difficulties were a sign of God's displeasure. There was great evidence to refute their claims and no evidence to support it, but they were sure they understood the situation.

As Job sat in a pile of ashes, covered with sores, having lost his wealth and his children, his friends added to his suffering. Sadly, many Christians make this same error in judgment, assuming that if something bad happens to a fellow believer, that believer must have done something to deserve it. For instance, they might suggest Christians who are sick don't have enough faith to be healed. Or they may gossip about parents with rebellious adult children, claiming they didn't raise them properly, even though they have no evidence to support such a claim.

God clearly rebuked Job's friends, saying, "You have not spoken the truth about me, as my servant Job has" (Job 42:7).

Some things happen because of an unhealthy or sinful action: a drunken driver hits a pedestrian, a smoker develops lung cancer, or a thief gets caught. But when there's no clear cause and effect, we shouldn't invent one. This is a time when "judge not!" applies.

Three Other Times to Say "Judge Not"

In Chapter 2, we'll see that the Bible offers clear criteria for judging people's behavior, but we don't have the ability to judge their motives. We can make educated guesses based on things they say and do, but we can't read their minds. Did they do something intentionally or accidentally? Did they fully understand the results or were they simply foolish?

We can't always know these answers. In addition, we are not aware of good things and bad things that people do in secret. The passage below addresses this type of judgment:

> Therefore judge nothing before the appointed time; wait until the Lord comes. He will bring to light what is hidden in darkness and will expose the motives of the heart. At that time each will receive their praise from God. (1 Cor. 4:5)

If this verse is taken out of context, people could use it to claim that we must not judge anything until Christ's return, but that would be another childish interpretation that ignores the context and denies other Scriptures about judgment. This verse specifically addresses those things we cannot fully understand because we are not all-knowing. Only our Lord is omniscient.

Another area where we're told to "judge not" is in the nonessentials of our faith. Romans 14:1–15:3 offers detailed advice about dealing with legitimate differences in the body of Christ, because we don't all apply scriptural principles in identical ways. However, these verses do not encourage us to accept false teachings.

Most aspects of our faith are non-negotiable. But for centuries, genuine believers have debated where God's sovereignty and man's free will intersect. They've held different views about spiritual gifts, church organization, and other practices.

> ***We must not judge people by externals such as appearance, position, wealth, education, or fame. These are worldly values, not God's values (1 John 2:15–17).***

We can hold tightly to our doctrines, but we must recognize that most nonessential doctrines involve some extrapolation of Scripture. On this side of heaven some mystery is involved in our faith. Instead of judging each other about these differences, this passage encourages us to show grace and love.

James 2:1–9 warns us against another form of ungodly judgment. We must not judge people by externals such as appearance, position, wealth, education, or fame. These are worldly values, not God's values (1 John 2:15–17).

In summary, there are some types of judgment that are not biblical, and it's appropriate in those cases to say, "Judge not!" But claiming that Christians are never supposed to judge sin or sinners clearly contradicts God's Word and purposes, as we will see in the following chapters.

Digging Deeper: Questions for Group or Personal Study

1. Matthew 7:1–5 specifically talks about judging others differently than we judge ourselves. What additional insights are found in Romans 2:1–4?

2. Have you ever had a "plank" in your eye that distorted your view of a particular situation? How did you handle it when you realized this problem?

3. Even when Christians judge sin and sinners in appropriate ways, we may face criticism. How does Jesus explain this problem in John 15:18–25? Have you encountered this problem in your life? If so, how have you handled it?

4. Why should Christians be better judges than unbelievers, according to First Corinthians 2:6–16?

5. Jeremiah 9:23–24 talks about correctly understanding God's character. Do you think the modern church understands that biblical love always includes justice and righteousness? How is our view of things altered by leaving these things out of our definition of love? How does it lead to misunderstandings about judgment?

6. Take some time to read Job and see how God helped Job readjust his confused thinking about his problems. Compare this with Paul's attitude toward his suffering and mistreatment in Philippians. How can these two books help you judge hardships more accurately?

2

Things We Are *Commanded* to Judge

NOW THAT WE have talked about inappropriate forms of judgment, let's talk about things we are *commanded* to judge, according to Scripture.

Judging Deception

Judging false teachings is an important aspect of Christian discernment (1 John 4:1; 1 Thess. 5:19–22). And Scripture tells us to judge the teacher as well as the teaching.

> Watch out for false prophets. They come to you in sheep's clothing, but inwardly they are ferocious wolves. By their fruit you will recognize them. Do people pick grapes from thornbushes, or figs from thistles? Likewise, every good tree bears good fruit, but a bad tree bears bad fruit. A good tree cannot bear bad fruit, and a bad tree cannot bear good fruit. Every tree that does not bear good fruit is cut down and thrown into the fire. Thus, by their fruit you will recognize them. (Matt. 7:15–20)

False teachings and false teachers are usually deceptively attractive. We need to be "fruit inspectors," identifying the fruit of a person's teachings and the fruit of their lives, determining if they represent biblical beliefs, purposes, and character.

> For of this you can be sure: No immoral, impure or greedy person—such a person is an idolater—has any inheritance in the kingdom

> of Christ and of God. Let no one deceive you with empty words, for because of such things God's wrath comes on those who are disobedient. Therefore do not be partners with them. (Eph. 5:5–7)

Judging Fellow Believers

Judging is a necessary and healthy aspect of Christian fellowship. We have a special responsibility to judge and confront fellow believers who behave in ungodly ways:

> If your brother or sister sins against you, rebuke them, and if they repent, forgive them. (Luke 17:3)
>
> Brothers and sisters, if someone is caught in a sin, you who live by the Spirit should restore that person gently. But watch yourselves, or you also may be tempted. (Gal. 6:1)
>
> My brothers and sisters, if one of you should wander from the truth and someone should bring that person back, remember this: Whoever turns a sinner from the error of their way will save them from death and cover over a multitude of sins. (James 5:19–20)
>
> Take special note of anyone who does not obey our instruction in this letter. Do not associate with them, in order that they may feel ashamed. Yet do not regard them as an enemy, but warn them as you would a fellow believer. (2 Thess. 3:14–15)

Many ministry leaders have gone to their ruin because others did not hold them accountable. No matter how mature we may be in our faith, we need to be confronted and corrected when we do something that is biblically inappropriate.

Christian "Body-Snatchers"

Did you know that Christians are actually commanded to be "body-snatchers"? Not the kind found in sci-fi films, but the kind found in Jude 1:22–23 (NLT): "You must show mercy to those whose faith is wavering. Rescue others by snatching them from the flames of judgment. Show mercy to still others, but do so with great caution, hating the sins that contaminate their lives."

Note the important points in this passage: Mercy is mentioned twice. Our motives matter. Are we interested in the well-being of those who are heading in the wrong direction—to the flames of judgment—or are we simply hoping to make ourselves look good?

Our goal should be to keep sinners from damaging their relationship with the Lord.

Judgment and mercy go hand in hand. We must hate the sin. We must be motivated by the knowledge that sin is destructive, brutal, evil, and damaging. Our goal should be to keep sinners from damaging their relationship with the Lord.

The verses before this passage in Jude help us understand what equips us to be "body-snatchers": "But you, dear friends, by building yourselves up in your most holy faith and praying in the Holy Spirit, keep yourselves in God's love as you wait for the mercy of our Lord Jesus Christ to bring you to eternal life" (Jude 1:20–21).

We cannot address others' sins if we are not walking with the Lord ourselves. This doesn't mean we must be perfect. If that were the requirement, no Christian would be able to correct another person. But we must be honestly dealing with our own sins so we can accurately recognize sin and offer an example to those who have strayed.

We need fellow believers to keep us on track with the Lord, and they need us. Sometimes that involves judging and correcting each other.

Formal Church Judgment

We should welcome everyone to our church, whether they are living godly or ungodly lifestyles. But church members should be believers who are seeking to follow Christ. That is the purpose of what is called formal church judgment or "church discipline."

> If your brother or sister sins, go and point out their fault, just between the two of you. If they listen to you, you have won them

> over. But if they will not listen, take one or two others along, so that "every matter may be established by the testimony of two or three witnesses." If they still refuse to listen, tell it to the church; and if they refuse to listen even to the church, treat them as you would a pagan or a tax collector. (Matt. 18:15–17)

Similar advice is given in First Corinthians 5:9–13. All Christians have sins to overcome, but formal church discipline is designed to address church members who are involved in sinful lifestyles. The body of Christ has a serious responsibility to keep church members and leaders accountable to biblical principles. Pastors, elders, deacons, and teachers must be above reproach (1 Tim. 3:1–12). No one living an ungodly lifestyle should be allowed to represent the church. If we overlook sinful lifestyles in church members, we can expect increased sinfulness in our congregation as a whole (1 Cor. 5:1–8).

This process is based on the clear teaching in Scripture that genuine believers will respond to church discipline because "No one who lives in [Christ] keeps on sinning. No one who continues to sin has either seen him or known him" (1 John 3:6). Those who refuse to repent prove they have no room in their hearts for God's Word (1:8–10).

The process of church discipline starts with private confrontation, which should prevent rumors and slander. It's a loving act meant to restore the sinning member to fellowship.

The discussion of formal church discipline in First Corinthians 5 concludes by saying, "What business is it of mine to judge those outside the church? Are you not to judge those inside? God will judge those outside. 'Expel the wicked person from among you'" (5:12–13).

If we take that verse out of context, it could lead to another half-truth belief—that it's not appropriate for us to judge non-Christians. But this statement applies to formal church discipline, not to all forms of judgment.

We judge ungodly behavior in unbelievers as well as believers. We should address it when it causes harm to others, and we might also address it when we share the gospel. But our perspective is different. We realize that until unbelievers are saved, they cannot accurately understand sin. We don't bring them before the church, because they are not church members.

Corrupt Fellowship

Friendships have a powerful influence on us. Our closest relationships should be with believers who are living their faith. That means we must judge people's character and lifestyle when developing friendships. "Do not be misled: 'Bad company corrupts good character'" (1 Cor. 15:33).

After my senior year in high school, I spent the summer working as a waitress. The staff in the restaurant used the F-word frequently. Even though I hadn't yet committed my life to Christ, I'd always found that word disgusting. But within a matter of weeks, it was part of my vocabulary. Bad company corrupts good character.

I saw this Scripture illustrated again a few months later when I started my freshman year of college at an out-of-state university where I didn't know a soul. A junior girl in my dorm asked me and several other freshmen girls to join her on an overnight trip to see the sights in the state capital.

It sounded fun, but it wasn't. That night I found myself in a hotel room filled with people I'd never met. I ended up sleeping under a desk with my face to the wall, protecting my eyes from both the immoral sexual activity in the room and the pungent marijuana smoke.

I wasn't a believer, but my momma was, and she'd shared enough wisdom with me to keep me from getting involved in any of those activities.

Sadly, the other freshmen girls who'd come to see the sights saw some sights they hadn't bargained for and learned some new ways to sin. I didn't realize it at the time, but I was getting a true-life illustration of First Corinthians 15:33. This older student was not good company for any of us.

We can't completely control our influences at work, at school, or in our neighborhood, but we must make sure that the major influences in our lives don't compromise our faith. And that requires judging people's values and behavior.

This doesn't mean we cut off family members who are ungodly. God placed us in our families, and He can teach us how to love relatives without being influenced by their bad values. But when it comes to friendships, we must choose friends who keep us on track with the Lord (Prov. 13:20). And when we are making decisions, we should seek godly counsel.

Furthermore, we don't form partnerships with nonbelievers because God Himself has judged all unbelievers unworthy of certain types of relationships with His people (2 Cor. 6:14–18). I recently saw the importance of this command illustrated when a well-known professing Christian chose business partners from the LDS church and started making public statements claiming Mormons worship the same Jesus Christians worship. Partnerships affect our discernment, our faith, and our actions.

Some situations occur in which we cannot completely avoid "bad company," but when we have the ability to choose, God wants us to choose like-minded believers for our closest influences. This is also why Christians should not date or marry non-Christians. This doesn't mean God wants us to divorce a non-Christian spouse. Once we are married, we must honor our commitment with God's help and wisdom (1 Cor. 7:12–16). But God wants His people to avoid the problems of "unequal yoking."

Judging Temptations

We've talked about judging bad companions and false teachings, but we also must judge other influences in our lives. Psalm 101:3 warns against entertaining ourselves with immorality:

I will not look with approval
  on anything that is vile.
I hate what faithless people do;
  I will have no part in it.

Television once set such high standards that bedroom scenes showed married couples in twin beds. Now, most entertainment not only includes immorality, it celebrates and glorifies it. Just as bad company corrupts good character, bad entertainment, music, and reading materials have played an enormous part in changing people's values.

If something is extremely popular with the world, there's a good chance it's based on deceptive philosophies.

Scripture warns us in First John 2:15–17, "Do not love the world or anything in the world. If anyone loves the world, love for the Father is not in them. For everything in the world—the lust of the flesh, the lust of the eyes, and the pride of life—comes not from the Father but from the world. The world and its desires pass away, but whoever does the will of God lives forever."

If something is extremely popular with the world, there's a good chance it's based on deceptive philosophies. This is even true when the content is described as "Christian." The path of true faith is narrow. Sound biblical truths don't appeal to fallen human nature. Typically, if a Christian book or show is extremely popular with non-Christians, there's a good chance it presents a half-truth gospel.

Another major problem is *syncretism*, which happens when Christians try to "Christianize" pagan practices. Throughout the Old Testament, the Israelites got into trouble by trying to merge their beliefs with those of the pagan nations around them.

The same thing happens today when Christians get involved with things like the Enneagram or yoga. Have you ever heard an exercise program praised with the same fervor and loyalty as yoga? It's staggering how many have tried to Christianize this Hindu ritual. This also illustrates the power and attraction pagan practices can have.

Satan is intent on stealing the hearts and minds of people (2 Cor. 4:4; 1 Pet. 5:8), and Christians are vulnerable when we fail to guard our hearts (Prov. 4:23). Scripture explains our responsibility: "Have nothing to do with the fruitless deeds of darkness, but rather expose them" (Eph. 5:11).

We must carefully judge all things biblically. "See to it that no one takes you captive through hollow and deceptive philosophy, which depends on human tradition and the elemental spiritual forces of this world rather than on Christ" (Col. 2:8).

Digging Deeper: Questions for Group or Personal Study

1. If we graciously and biblically confront someone about their sin and they refuse to listen, what comfort can we find in Ezekiel 33:1–16?

2. Consider ways that you can respond if you are appropriately addressing sin, and a fellow believer says, "It's not our place to judge." How might Ephesians 5:8–13 and Romans 1:16–18 help you respond?

3. Have you evaluated your friendships and honestly considered whether any of your friends are the kind described in First Corinthians 15:33?

4. What insights do we gain about godly correction from Psalm 141:5 and Proverbs 9:8?

5. Do you think most Christians understand the serious nature of sin? What insights can we gain from James 4:9–10 and Isaiah 66:2?

3

Considerations When Judging

BESIDES UNDERSTANDING the specific things we are supposed to judge, we must also be sensitive to other things that impact appropriate biblical judgments.

Our Job and the Spirit's Job

We've talked about our responsibility to confront fellow believers who are involved in unrepentant sins so they can experience the refreshment and protection of repentance and forgiveness. We should make sure we explain our concerns using Scripture, so they know we are not simply sharing our opinions. And we should approach them as graciously as possible, letting them know we care about them.

> And the Lord's servant must not be quarrelsome but must be kind to everyone, able to teach, not resentful. Opponents must be gently instructed, in the hope that God will grant them repentance leading them to a knowledge of the truth, and that they will come to their senses and escape from the trap of the devil, who has taken them captive to do his will. (2 Tim. 2:24–26)

However, even if we do things scripturally, some people will stubbornly refuse to repent, and we're not responsible for their decision. In fact, if they are divisive, Scripture tells us to warn them twice. If we see no results, we should move on (Titus 3:10).

Putting First Things First When We Judge

Jesus commands us to share the gospel, calling people to repentance and salvation (Matt. 4:17, 28:18–20; Mark 1:14–15; Acts 2:38). We must never be afraid to address sin, but we must be careful to put first things first. Unbelievers are incapable of fully understanding their sins until they understand the gospel (1 Cor. 2:14).

When my husband and I were in Christian ministry overseas, we frequented a sandwich shop, and we liked engaging the owner in conversation. She enjoyed talking with us, and we often had opportunities to share things about our faith in Christ.

Sadly, she had a terrible habit of using profanity. Her language made us uncomfortable, but we felt the Lord didn't want us to address it with her at that time. This woman's problem wasn't language—it was her need for Christ.

We have a responsibility to correct Christians who use profanity. And it might be appropriate to ask non-Christians not to use bad language in our presence. In fact, in some cases, graciously addressing a person's profanity might be the starting point for sharing Christ. But sometimes God may have us wait before addressing an unbeliever's sins. It's a matter of being sensitive to the Holy Spirit.

Indirect Judgment

As a new Christian, I looked forward to watching my favorite soap opera. I felt a twinge of conscience when the storyline became immoral, but I kept watching.

One day, in my women's Bible study, a friend talked about being convicted that she shouldn't watch soap operas. God used her testimony to convict me. The following day I sat in front of the TV at the usual time, but I couldn't bring myself to turn it on.

My friend's conviction had become mine. This is an important aspect of our fellowship with other believers. We might call it "indirect judgment" or "peer mentoring."

Even though my friend shared her conviction sincerely and humbly, in some settings, she might have been corrected for judging others in our group who watched soap operas. It's easy to become defensive when someone addresses something that hits close to home. But sharing our convictions is appropriate, and I'm grateful for the times I've been judged and counseled indirectly by the godliness of fellow believers. As Paul counseled Timothy, "Set an example for the believers in speech, in conduct, in love, in faith and in purity" (1 Tim. 4:12).

Dealing with Unloving Rebukes

When my son was in his early twenties, an older man in our church rebuked him for having a bad attitude. This man had shown no interest in our son, nor had he taken time to know him, and most of his rebuke was built on misunderstandings.

However, our son responded respectfully, and when he explained the situation to me, he said, "He didn't do it in a very loving way, but there's some truth in what he said, and I need to take it to heart."

I was proud of my son's biblical response to harsh correction because it's rare in our culture.

> ***Sadly, culture has influenced many Christians to reject criticism, even when given in love.***

If we need to rebuke someone, we should do our best to speak the truth in love, being gracious and thoughtful (Gal. 6:1; Eph. 4:15; 1 Thess. 5:14). But that doesn't mean we should refuse valid criticism just because it's poorly expressed.

Sadly, culture has influenced many Christians to reject criticism, even when given in love. Many people believe that parents, teachers, family, and friends should give them a continual diet of praise and affirmation. But our culture reveals how unhealthy undeserved approval can be. It has led to an increase in narcissistic attitudes, discontent, blame-shifting, and a victim mentality, in which any disagreement is interpreted as hate.

The best way to love fellow believers is to help them recognize that their sins are harmful to their lives and their witness.

Unsanctified Grace

Years ago, while working with a group of Christians, I realized that one person had trouble getting along with several people on the team. I'd been praying about whether or not I should say something to her. Then, one afternoon when we gathered for prayer, I discovered that she had already been hearing the conviction of God's Spirit. She explained that God had shown her that she had been jealous of some of the team members, and she'd been acting selfishly.

I was blessed to be reminded of the wonderful conviction of God's Spirit. Hearing someone humbly confess their sins encourages us to do the same.

But this woman's repentant words were barely out of her mouth when several team members doused her sincere confession with "unsanctified grace." They knew nothing about the tension she had caused, and, thinking they were being "nice," they told her that she was being too hard on herself.

Sadly, instead of showing this woman love, they actually encouraged her to ignore the Holy Spirit's conviction. As you can imagine, this complicated the situation, leaving the repentant woman confused.

We should always be ready to comfort and encourage people, but we must be careful to never interfere with the convicting work of God's Spirit.

Digging Deeper: Questions for Group or Personal Study

1. Galatians 6:1 warns us to be careful when confronting a sinning brother so we will not be tempted. How might this tempt us? How might we avoid these temptations?

2. Ephesians 4:15 tells us to speak the truth in love. How does the world's view of love differ from the biblical view? These passages offer some insights: Second Timothy 2:24–26; Titus 3:9–11; Ephesians 5:8–13.

3. Many years ago, I misjudged a fellow believer and unfairly criticized him. Sadly, it took me several years to realize my sin. Despite the time that had elapsed, I knew I needed to contact him, admit my sin, and ask his forgiveness which he graciously gave me. Have you unfairly judged someone whom you need to contact?

4

"Judge Not" Misunderstandings

IF WE TRY TO correct someone's false views of judging, we might encounter these additional half-truth arguments. Let's be prepared to answer them.

Misunderstandings about Condemnation

Even if you judge something biblically, you're bound to hear someone say, "If Jesus didn't judge people, neither should we." This claim is based on John 3:17 (NASB): "For God did not send the Son into the world to judge the world, but that the world might be saved through Him."

However, when we study the immediate context of John 3:17, we discover that Jesus judged sinners in the very next verses (3:18–21). Then, a few chapters later, Christ said, "For judgment I have come into this world" (9:39). In addition, throughout the Gospels, Christ judged people. This may sound contradictory, but it's not.

This half-truth is based on a misunderstanding about condemnation (final judgment) and earthly judgment. In fact, most Bible translations use the word "condemn" instead of "judge" in John 3:17. Christ didn't come to earth to condemn us to hell. He came to offer us the hope of salvation, addressing and judging our sins and offering us forgiveness.

Ironically, another popular "judge not" rebuke uses an opposite strategy, claiming "It's God's place to judge people, not ours." It's true that only God can judge perfectly and pass final judgment (condemnation) on a person. But He commands us throughout Scripture to judge people biblically. And since God tells us it's our place to judge, then it's our place to judge.

Judge the Sin, Not the Sinner?

We've all heard the statement, "Hate the sin; love the sinner." That's true. In fact, helping a sinner turn from their sins is the most loving thing we can do (James 5:19–20).

But sometimes this statement is used to promote a "no-fault" attitude toward sin. Sometimes the underlying message of this statement is, "Judge the sin, not the sinner."

Of course, that's neither logical nor biblical. We can't separate the sin from the sinner because sin doesn't just happen to us, we choose it (1:14–15).

> ***We must not downplay, shift blame, excuse, ignore, or justify our sins or the sins of others.***

When we become Christians, our sins—past, present, and future—are paid for by Christ's death. But part of growing in Christ is understanding the serious nature of sin and dealing with our sins deliberately (1 John 2:3–6; Eph. 5:1–20). We must not downplay, shift blame, excuse, ignore, or justify our sins or the sins of others.

> If we claim to be without sin, we deceive ourselves and the truth is not in us. If we confess our sins, he is faithful and just and will forgive us our sins and purify us from all unrighteousness. If we claim we have not sinned, we make him out to be a liar and his word is not in us. (1 John 1:8–10)

Our culture is more offended by judgment than by sin. But we have a responsibility to be salt and light, properly judging ourselves and judging fellow believers in appropriate ways (Matt. 5:13–16).

"It's Not Our Business What Other People Do"

While scanning items at a self-check-out, I noticed the man next to me was throwing unscanned items into his bags. I could have responded to his theft in different ways. I could have used situational ethics and assumed he was in genuine need, deciding it was okay for him to steal. Or I could have decided it wasn't my place to report him—after all, he wasn't stealing from me. Or I could have decided that the store was big enough to handle the small losses he was causing. And of course, I could always have claimed that "It's not my place to judge."

The "judge not" half-truth can come in very handy when we want to ignore our responsibilities. However, if I'd used any of these excuses, I'd have become a partner in this man's crime.

Romans 13:1–5 tells us to be subject to governing authorities, not only to keep from being arrested ourselves, but also "as a matter of conscience." Our job is not to excuse or justify crime. Our job is to recognize it for what it is and do the right thing, even when it makes us uncomfortable.

I knew what I had to do, so I informed the clerk, and she "helped" the thief scan the unscanned items in his bags. He got off easier with her than he did with God.

"You Pharisee!"

If we seek to judge people and things biblically, graciously, and appropriately, we may still be called a "Pharisee." This is a common rebuke based on a lack of knowledge.

Christ often rebuked the Pharisees, but it wasn't because they spoke about God's commands and sought to warn people about sins that would damage their souls. Christ rebuked the Pharisees because of their self-promotion, hypocritical judgment, and their focus on human traditions (Matt. 23).

Unlike the Pharisees, Christ called people to genuine repentance (4:17; 11:20; Luke 13:3). That's why people hated Him. In a conversation with His unbelieving brothers, Christ said, "The world cannot hate you, but it hates me because I testify that its works are evil" (John 7:7).

Jesus also spoke of the reason we are unjustly criticized for speaking truth:

> If the world hates you, keep in mind that it hated me first. If you belonged to the world, it would love you as its own. As it is, you do not belong to the world, but I have chosen you out of the world. That is why the world hates you. Remember what I told you: "A servant is not greater than his master." If they persecuted me, they will persecute you also. If they obeyed my teaching, they will obey yours also. (15:18–20)

The Woman Caught in Adultery

The story of the woman caught in adultery is important to mention at this point because it's often used to justify the "judge not" half-truth.

Before we address this Bible passage (John 8:1–11), it's important to note that this story isn't found in the oldest available manuscripts of the Bible and could have been added by a scribe. The one thing that might cause us to doubt its authenticity is the way it is so often misused and misunderstood. But the passage doesn't contradict scriptural principles, and it's worth addressing because it has become a part of Christian thinking.

For some reason, many people have come to believe that Jesus didn't judge the woman in this passage. So let's take a closer look.

The men in John 8 were not really seeking to have the adulterous woman stoned to death. Their target was Jesus. "They were using this question as a trap, in order to have a basis for accusing him" (John 8:6).

The Romans were the only ones who could have someone put to death, and it required a trial. If Jesus said she should be stoned, they would have accused Him of sedition or inciting rebellion against authorities. If Jesus said she should not be stoned, they would have accused Him of ignoring God's Old Testament commands (Lev. 20:10).

Jesus judged the men indirectly, helping them face their hypocrisy by saying that those without sin could throw the first stone. Was this Christ's way of saying that only perfect people can confront others about their sins? No. We're all imperfect and as we've seen, multiple Scriptures command us to judge people. But these men were not in a position to judge this woman because they had sinful intents against Jesus, and they had no regard for the woman.

Jesus told the woman that He didn't condemn her to be stoned, but He clearly judged her when He said, "Go now and leave your life of sin" (John 8:11).

His purpose with both the men and the woman was to bring them to salvation, not condemn them. His treatment of the men was unique in that He let them judge themselves. But He judged the woman directly, identifying her as someone living a sinful life. We can conclude from this passage that under the New Covenant, Jesus doesn't believe people should be stoned to death for adultery. But we can't use this passage to claim that Christ didn't judge the woman.

True Love Hates Sin

The popularity of the "judge not" movement is related to our world's casual attitude toward sin. When people accept cultural values, they lose their ability to judge sin accurately. But

Christians know that God is a loving Father. His instructions for our lives are given for our protection and well-being. The most loving thing we can do is to hate sin and warn others of its damage.

> Love must be sincere. Hate what is evil; cling to what is good. (Rom. 12:9)
>
> Let those who love the LORD hate evil. (Ps. 97:10)
>
> Carefully determine what pleases the Lord. Take no part in the worthless deeds of evil and darkness; instead, expose them. It is shameful even to talk about the things that ungodly people do in secret. But their evil intentions will be exposed when the light shines on them . . . So be careful how you live. Don't live like fools, but like those who are wise. (Eph. 5:10–15, NLT)

These are strong commands. We don't accept, excuse, downplay, or minimize sin. We hate it, refuse to be involved in it, and we judge it in appropriate ways.

The Most Ironic Hypocrisy

Unrepentant sin obstructs our view of right and wrong. We've all heard of pastors who had immoral relationships while preaching biblical morality or people who embezzled funds while writing about financial integrity. But "eye plank" hypocrisy is a serious problem—even when it happens on a smaller scale:

- Rude and insensitive persons who claim that others are rude and insensitive.
- People who claim they can't tolerate Christians because they aren't tolerant.
- Disrespectful adult children who claim that their parents don't respect them enough.

But let me explain the most ironic hypocrisy of all: When someone claims it's wrong to judge, but they judge anyone who judges biblically! If they truly believe it's wrong to judge, this violates their own belief and provides a perfect example of the hypocritical judgment described in Matthew 7:1–5.

We must understand the bottom line of biblical judgment: Everyone judges people. Some do it biblically and some don't.

Uncharted Territory

I'd like to add an additional reason why the "judge not" half-truth is harmful to the Christian community. A few years ago, I was part of a conversation that reflected a common trend. A fellow believer explained that a family member had chosen an LGBTQ+ lifestyle. Before she had an opportunity to explain her concerns, a well-meaning Christian changed the subject by saying, "Well, it's not our place to judge. It's our place to love."

> ***Biblical judgment is loving. Nothing is loving about letting people walk blindly down destructive paths away from God.***

This so clearly shows our problem. We can bring up the sin of gossip, and it's unlikely anyone will use the "judge not" rebuke. However, we often hear this rebuke when we mention a sin that is approved and celebrated by our culture. This puts us at a disadvantage, missing opportunities to discuss these influences biblically. It's a sign that we've bought into the cultural definition of love and discarded the biblical definition.

We must understand that biblical judgment is loving. Nothing is loving about letting people walk blindly down destructive paths away from God.

We need God's Word, prayer, and open discussion as we face new challenges from our culture. People need to express their sadness and concerns and ask questions without being cut off by "judge not" rhetoric.

Digging Deeper: Questions for Group or Personal Study

1. What insights do we get about self-justification from Proverbs 16:2 and 21:2?
2. How do Second Corinthians 4:4 and John 10:10 help us understand why the "judge not" half-truth has become so popular?
3. If you have a group of Christian friends who are mature enough to learn some hard truths, I suggest this "experiment." Choose one of the sins from First Corinthians 6:9–10, such as greed. Bring up your concern with the increase in greed in our world, and note your friends' responses. At another time, bring up your concern about the increase in LGBTQ+ lifestyles, and note the responses. If greed receives a normal response but LGBTQ+ lifestyles evoke sympathy, "judge not" rhetoric, and stories of mistreatment of homosexuals, it might be time for your group to study Romans 1.
4. When talking about the man who was shoplifting, I explained the command in Romans 13:1–5 about obeying government authority. How does Acts 4:8–20 provide a limit to that obedience for Christians living in persecuted countries? Can you think of other examples when Christians should disobey a government law?

5. Christ clearly explained that He was hated by the world (John 7:7) and that His true followers would be hated by the world (15:18–20). Why do you think non-Christians so often claim that Christ was a nonconfrontational person who loved people instead of judging them?
6. What important aspect of Leviticus 20:10 did the men ignore when they brought the woman to Jesus in John 8:1–11?

Section

2

Half-Truths that Exalt Human Desires

A number of half-truths are related to our culture's serious misunderstandings about our fallen human nature. We must understand that only God's ways and God's wisdom are perfect. And we must realize that His mercy to us is totally undeserved. Our world tends to exalt mankind, and this attitude has crept into the church.

5

Half-Truth: "Our Well-Being Depends on High Self-Esteem"

WE DO NEED TO HAVE confidence to fulfill God's purposes and speak up for His principles, but this must flow from our trust in God, not trust in ourselves. We need an honest, humble view of ourselves, not an inflated view.

There was a time when people admired humility and self-sacrifice. For the most part, Christians and non-Christians alike agreed with the wisdom of Proverbs 11:2: "Pride leads to disgrace, but with humility comes wisdom" (NLT).

But in the 1980s, attitudes began to change. Secular psychologists successfully convinced the masses that high self-esteem was our greatest human need. Parents were persuaded that their children would be emotionally damaged if they didn't feed them a constant diet of praise and affirmation. Many schools decided that grading students was harmful for their well-being, and sports teams began giving trophies to all team members, no matter how poorly they played.

But this philosophy wasn't limited to children. It quickly caught on with all age groups because it brought out the desires of our sinful human nature.

Pride has always been one of our greatest enemies. It damages relationships, wrecks marriages, and endangers our culture with crime and violence. But worst of all, it keeps us from repenting and turning to God. And, as is often the case, when something is popular in culture, it creeps into the church, contaminating Christian thinking.

Twisting the Second Greatest Command

To convince Christians that self-esteem was one of our greatest needs, people began redefining Scripture passages. For example, in Matthew 22:36–40 when Jesus was asked which was the greatest commandment, He replied, "'Love the Lord your God with all your heart and with all your soul and with all your mind.' This is the first and greatest commandment. And the second is like it: 'Love your neighbor as yourself.' All the Law and the Prophets hang on these two commandments."

Christian self-esteem advocates began using this passage to claim that in order to love others, we must first love ourselves. So, let's step back and analyze that claim carefully.

Loving our neighbors isn't about affirming them and building their self-esteem. It's about treating them fairly and humanely.

If loving ourselves was a truly important problem for us, Jesus wouldn't have used it in this verse as an example of how to love others. And loving our neighbors isn't about affirming them and building their self-esteem. It's about treating them fairly and humanely.

We "love" ourselves enough to be fed, clothed, and protected, and we should have this kind of love for all people, even our enemies, whom we don't respect: "If your enemy is hungry, feed him; if he is thirsty, give him something to drink. . . . Do not be overcome by evil, but overcome evil with good" (Rom. 12:20–21).

The Greatest Commandment also provides an important difference between the love we have for God and the love we have for others. Jesus didn't tell us to love God as we love ourselves. Our love for God should be different from our self-love and from our love for our neighbors. It should be wholehearted, including trust, esteem, honor, worship, and obedience.

In some ways, the self-esteem movement has rewritten the Greatest Commandment, encouraging us to love and esteem ourselves as we would love and esteem God. And that denies a basic scriptural truth: "God opposes the proud but shows favor to the humble" (1 Pet. 5:5; James 4:6).

Philippians 2:3–4 further destroys self-esteem teachings when it says, "Do nothing out of selfish ambition or vain conceit. Rather, in humility value others above yourselves, not looking to your own interests but each of you to the interests of the others."

But it doesn't stop there. The following verses in Philippians 2 offer Christ as our example: God became man and sacrificed Himself for sinful humanity.

Christ deserved esteem, but He didn't seek it. Instead, He humbled Himself and allowed Himself to be despised, mistreated, rebuked, mocked, and crucified for the purposes of God. This and many other passages completely deny self-esteem philosophies.

Self-Esteem's Twisted Proverb

Another verse that has been adopted by self-esteem advocates is Proverbs 23:7 (KJV): "As he thinketh in his heart, so is he."

This phrase is often quoted to "prove" that we should think highly of ourselves because what we think about ourselves is what we become. However, to have this meaning, this verse must be cut in half, taken out of context and only quoted in the King James Version.

The full verse in the KJV reads: "For as he thinketh in his heart, so is he: Eat and drink, saith he to thee; but his heart is not with thee."

This proverb is about the thoughts of a stingy man, not about self-esteem. If you read this verse in other translations, the meaning becomes even clearer. For example, the NIV says: "For he is the kind of person / who is always thinking about the cost. / 'Eat and drink,' he says to you, / but his heart is not with you."

Feelings of superiority are based on a false view of self. I might have such high self-esteem that I think I'm a writer in the same league as C.S. Lewis. But that wouldn't make me such a writer; it would make me an arrogant fool. And that's exactly what we're encouraging our children to be when we teach them to think highly of themselves.

Turning a Psalm Upside Down

One day I decided to listen to an online sermon from a well-known teacher who represents the "Christian" self-esteem movement. I wanted to see if criticisms of his beliefs were legitimate.

This pastor encouraged his congregation to say positive things about themselves. But Scripture says the opposite: "Let someone else praise you, and not your own mouth; / an outsider, and not your own lips" (Prov. 27:2).

Next, he quoted Psalm 139:13–14: "For you created my inmost being; / you knit me together in my mother's womb. / I praise you because I am fearfully and wonderfully made; / your works are wonderful, / I know that full well."

But instead of seeing the passage's obvious message, the preacher said these verses were a perfect example of self-praise because David was telling the world he was amazing and wonderful.

Of course, there's no truth in this claim. This pastor completely missed the point. David wasn't praising himself; he was praising God! He was expressing his awe of God's amazing creation design. His awe in Psalm 139 is similar to his awe in Psalm 8:4, where he said, "What is mankind that you are mindful of them, / human beings that you care for them?"

David was amazed that such an awesome God cares so much for sinful mankind that He created us in His image and gave us authority on earth.

Sometimes Christians think that because Christ died for us, we are worthy of His sacrifice. But that turns the meaning of grace upside down. None of us is worthy of God's incredible salvation and love. It's a totally undeserved gift of grace.

Humility is Not Self-Hatred

The Bible teaches neither self-love nor self-hatred. Instead, it commands us to have a realistic view of ourselves based on biblical principles of faith: "For by the grace given me I say to every one of you: Do not think of yourself more highly than you ought, but rather think of yourself with sober judgment, in accordance with the faith God has distributed to each of you" (Rom. 12:3).

> ***Whether a person suffers from high self-esteem or low self-esteem, the cure is the same: Quit focusing on self and start focusing on God and others in appropriate ways.***

Seeing ourselves realistically means acknowledging our weaknesses, sins, and failures as well as our strengths and successes. It means that when we sin, we genuinely repent without excuses or blame-shifting. And this is a bottom-line truth Christians need to grasp: Whether a person is suffering from high self-esteem or low self-esteem, the cure is the same: Quit focusing on self and start focusing on God and others in appropriate ways.

The Results

Secular psychology is deeply invested in promoting self-esteem teachings and creating additional false philosophies to help with the extra problems it causes. For several generations, parents have focused more on praising their children than on training them.

We have many self-assured adults who haven't learned self-control, have difficulty being corrected, and are dissatisfied with anything that doesn't bring them regular affirmation. They feel entitled to special treatment even when they've done nothing to deserve it.

Self-esteem also promotes selfishness and a love for pleasure and money. It makes people unashamed to boast, and it makes them less grateful and more demanding. It also promotes a victim mentality. Instead of learning how to get along with people, many self-assured adults blame-shift their problems onto others. This is especially true regarding adult children blaming parents instead of honoring them. That's one reason our culture is dealing with a pandemic of relationship problems and estrangements.

When Scripture describes moral decline, these things are part of it:

> But mark this: There will be terrible times in the last days. People will be lovers of themselves, lovers of money, boastful, proud, abusive, disobedient to their parents, ungrateful, unholy, without love, unforgiving, slanderous, without self-control, brutal, not lovers of the good, treacherous, rash, conceited, lovers of pleasure rather than lovers of God—having a form of godliness but denying its power. Have nothing to do with such people. (2 Tim. 3:1–5)

The Hatred of Correction

Even when correction is honest and constructive, many in the church view it negatively. The self-esteem movement and the "judge not" movement have encouraged many Christians to view God as soft on sin, always affirming, and never rebuking or disciplining us. It's not unusual to hear Christians claim that when God looks at them, He doesn't see their sins; He only sees Jesus.

It's true that when we follow Christ, our sins are completely forgiven, but God isn't ignorant of our sins nor is He content with our sinful character. God "disciplines those he loves, and he punishes each one he accepts as his child" (Heb. 12:6, NLT). This truth is also found in Revelation 3:19 when Jesus says, "Those whom I love I rebuke and discipline. So be earnest and repent."

Second Timothy 3:16–18 tells us, "All Scripture is God-breathed and is useful for teaching, rebuking, correcting and training in righteousness, so that the servant of God may be thoroughly equipped for every good work." God corrects and rebukes us as a loving Father (Heb. 12:4–13). When people buy into self-esteem beliefs, they forfeit personal growth that comes from correction. And Scripture doesn't sugarcoat their problem: "Whoever loves discipline loves knowledge, / but whoever hates correction is stupid" (Prov. 12:1).

Scriptural Examples

Scripture also offers specific examples in regard to self-esteem. Let's look at four:

Moses

Numbers 12:3 tells us that, "Moses was a very humble man, more humble than anyone else on the face of the earth."

But early in his adult life, Moses had high self-esteem, thinking his position in the royal court gave him a right to kill an Egyptian who was mistreating a fellow Israelite (Exod. 2:11–15). Moses' pride sent him into exile in Midian.

By the time God revealed Himself to Moses forty years later in the burning bush, Moses had obviously learned humility. In fact, he'd lost all confidence in himself, explaining to God that he wasn't adequate to lead (3:11). This tells us that God can use people who lack self-confidence, as long as they have confidence in God. With God's assurance and help, Moses became a great leader.

The Pharisees

The modern church uses the term "Pharisee" to criticize people who are legalistic or hypocritical. The Pharisees had those bad qualities, but their main problem was their desire for personal esteem. They weren't jealous for God's laws and commands. They were jealous for their own power and respect. They had extremely high self-esteem, and they expected others to esteem them. Christ's words in Matthew 23:5–7 make this clear:

> Everything they do is done for people to see: They make their phylacteries wide and the tassels on their garments long; they love the place of honor at banquets and the most important seats in the synagogues; they love to be greeted with respect in the marketplaces and to be called "Rabbi" by others.

The Centurion

In Matthew 8:5–13, when the Roman centurion asked Christ to heal his servant, Jesus offered to come with him and do it. The centurion responded by saying, "Lord, I do not deserve to have you come under my roof. But just say the word, and my servant will be healed" (8:8).

He explained that it was enough for Jesus to simply speak the healing. "When Jesus heard this, he was amazed and said to those following him, 'Truly I tell you, I have not found anyone in Israel with such great faith' " (8:10).

Imagine having faith that amazed Jesus!

This centurion perceived his unworthiness before the perfect Son of God. He amazed Jesus with his humility, respect, and understanding of Christ's power and position.

Today's culture would probably have assured the centurion he was worthy of Christ's help and rebuked him for speaking so poorly of himself. We need to remember that the meaning of grace is "undeserved favor." We are unworthy sinners who deserve eternal death, but Christ, in His grace and mercy, died to give us eternal life.

Dorcas

Bold evangelists and gifted teachers typically get the most attention in Christian circles, and this is one reason they have more difficulty maintaining a humble, honest attitude. If they aren't careful, their high self-esteem will make them think they are above the commands they teach.

On the other hand, humble servants often go unnoticed because they typically have modest views of themselves. I believe this is why the example of Dorcas is included in God's divinely inspired Word (Acts 9:36–43). She wasn't in the forefront. Instead, she put her faith to work behind the scenes, doing good deeds and helping the poor.

Scripture gives us an interesting view of her ministry by letting us "attend" her funeral, where a group of poor widows gathered to mourn her death, bringing articles of clothing Dorcas had made for them. But it gets even more interesting: Dorcas was able to speak to the guests at her own funeral because God used Peter to breathe life back into her dead body. God obviously wanted to call attention to this behind-the-scenes, servant evangelist. She was a striking example of a humble Christian whom God lifted up.

> ***Living for Christ is a wonderful opportunity and a serious responsibility. It brings us many blessings, but it's about self-denial, not self-esteem.***

What Scripture Says About Self

Scripture couldn't be clearer. Christians are called to humbly bring glory to God. Matthew 5:16 doesn't say, "Let your light shine before others, that they may see your good deeds and glorify you." It says, "Let your light shine before others, that they may see your good deeds and glorify your Father in heaven."

Living for Christ is a wonderful opportunity and a serious responsibility. It brings us many blessings, but it's about self-denial, not self-esteem. In Matthew 16:24–27, Jesus said,

> Whoever wants to be my disciple must deny themselves and take up their cross and follow me. For whoever wants to save their life will lose it, but whoever loses their life for me will find it. What good will it be for someone to gain the whole world, yet forfeit their soul? Or what can anyone give in exchange for their soul? For the Son of Man is going to come in his Father's glory with his angels, and then he will reward each person according to what they have done.

Esteeming ourselves, or seeking esteem from others, contradicts the Christian mission. Only when we esteem God can we have a realistic view of ourselves. The Christian life isn't about us. It's about our Lord. It's about following Christ and seeking spiritual rewards, not earthly ones.

We've addressed several verses in Philippians 2 as they relate to self-esteem, so let's summarize this section with verses 1–11:

> Therefore if you have any encouragement from being united with Christ, if any comfort from his love, if any common sharing in the Spirit, if any tenderness and compassion, then make my joy complete by being like-minded, having the same love, being one in spirit and of one mind. Do nothing out of selfish ambition or vain conceit. Rather, in humility value others above yourselves, not looking to your own interests but each of you to the interests of the others.
>
> In your relationships with one another, have the same mindset as Christ Jesus:
>
> Who, being in very nature God,
> did not consider equality with God something
> to be used to his own advantage;
> rather, he made himself nothing
> by taking the very nature of a servant,
> being made in human likeness.

And being found in appearance as a man,
  he humbled himself
  by becoming obedient to death—
    even death on a cross!

Therefore God exalted him to the highest place
  and gave him the name that is above every name,
that at the name of Jesus every knee should bow,
  in heaven and on earth and under the earth,
and every tongue acknowledge that Jesus Christ is Lord,
  to the glory of God the Father.

Digging Deeper: Questions for Group or Personal Study

1. Using Matthew 26:47–75 and Philippians 2, list some of the many ways Jesus humbled Himself for you and me.

2. Suppose someone excuses a person's sinful behavior by blaming it on a lack of self-esteem. How could you answer them using the principles in these verses: Proverbs 16:18; Luke 14:11; James 1:14–15; Ephesians 2:1–3?

3. How does Matthew 5:43–48 further explain the meaning of loving others as we love ourselves?

4. How does First John 2:15–17 speak to the truths in this chapter? What additional wisdom does it provide?

5. The self-esteem movement seeks to encourage people with sayings such as:
    - Trust your heart.
    - Follow your heart.
    - Believe in yourself.
    - Respect yourself, and others will respect you.
    - Tell yourself that you're amazing.
    - Don't let anyone make you feel bad about yourself.
    - What others think of you isn't as important as what you think of yourself.

    How would Scripture judge such statements?

6. This chapter shares several passages that refute self-esteem philosophy, but there are others. Keep a list of other passages when you are reading Scripture.

6

Half-Truth: "We Only Honor Parents Who Are Worthy of Honor"

OUR WORLD FACES AN epidemic of broken family relationships. Some statistics show that as many as 25 percent of American adults are estranged from their parents, with the children most often initiating separation.

The self-esteem movement helped create this problem by making people feel they deserve parents who constantly praise, support, and affirm them. The psychology of boundaries followed close behind this movement to encourage judgmental ultimatums.

If you look for resources on parent-child estrangements, you'll find many of them blame parents and sympathize with the adult children. But let's look at this issue logically and biblically, not culturally.

The Command

> Children, obey your parents in the Lord, for this is right. "Honor your father and mother"—which is the first commandment with a promise—"so that it may go well with you and that you may enjoy long life on the earth." (Eph. 6:1–3)

This command includes no age limit, but the type of obedience commanded in verse 1 obviously changes when children become adults and marry or live on their own. Those who marry start a new family with the new husband as the head (Gen. 2:24; Matt. 19:4–6). And adult children who are no longer dependent on their parents are also free to make their own decisions based on God's purposes.

> ***Honor is more than mere respect. It requires an attitude that mirrors obedience, even when a person becomes an adult.***

Yet, passages like Second Timothy 3:1–5 speak of ungodly adults who are "disobedient to their parents." This doesn't mean adult children must obey their parents' commands, but it offers an additional understanding of what it means to honor.

Honor is more than mere respect. It requires an attitude that mirrors obedience, even when a person becomes an adult.

A Misused Proverb and Old Testament Warning

One thing that fuels criticism of parents is a half-truth understanding of Proverbs 22:6 (KJV): "Train up a child in the way he should go: and when he is old, he will not depart from it."

Early in my Christian life, I heard this proverb used to assure parents that their children would grow up to be good Christians if they raised them properly. The flip side of this belief was reinforced by quoting one of several Old Testament verses such as Numbers 14:18, which says God "punishes the children for the sin of the parents to the third and fourth generation."

Many people use these passages to claim that parents are responsible for the faith and character of their adult children. However, as I grew in my faith, I met godly Christian couples with ungodly adult children, and there was every indication that they'd done their best to raise their children in the Lord.

When I researched this popular claim about Proverbs 22:6, I learned that Proverbs is a divinely inspired book of wisdom sayings (Prov. 1:1–6). If we claim all statements in Proverbs as promises, we'll have some strange doctrines. For example, we'll determine a person's godliness by the length of their life, because Proverbs 10:27 says, "The fear of the Lord adds length to life, but the years of the wicked are cut short."

Blaming parents for their adult child's sinful choices contradicts multiple Bible passages. The consistent teaching of Scripture is that each person is responsible for their own sinful choices.

Parents should seek to be godly examples because God will judge them if they are selfish, abusive, or negligent (Eph. 6:4; Col. 3:21). But parents are not responsible for their adult children's choices, actions, attitudes, and lifestyles. If we hold parents responsible for their adult children's actions, we can all blame our sins on our parents.

What about verses such as Numbers 14:18 that say children will be punished for their parents' sins? Apparently, Old Testament Israelites also misunderstood this statement, because in Ezekiel 18:1–4 God said to them,

> The word of the LORD came to me: "What do you people mean by quoting this proverb about the land of Israel:
>
> " 'The parents eat sour grapes,
> and the children's teeth are set on edge'?
>
> "As surely as I live, declares the Sovereign LORD, you will no longer quote this proverb in Israel. For everyone belongs to me, the parent as well as the child—both alike belong to me. The one who sins is the one who will die."

At the end of that chapter, God further clarified, "The child will not be punished for the parent's sins, and the parent will not be punished for the child's sins. Righteous people will be rewarded for their own righteous behavior, and wicked people will be punished for their own wickedness" (18:20, NLT).

This passage may sound as if it contradicts Numbers 14:18, but it actually clarifies it. Children often adopt the sinful practices of their parents, thus creating a sinful family legacy. But Ezekiel 18:20 assures us that each person is responsible for their behavior and any son or daughter can break a sinful family legacy by making godly choices.

The Irony and Hypocrisy of Estrangements

Sometimes a parent is genuinely abusive, and in those situations, children must treat the relationship carefully, never putting themselves in harm's way, seeking to forgive, and getting mature Christian counsel in handling the relationship. But statistics show that child abuse affects only a small percentage of people. The real problem is that many adult children set unreasonable standards for their parents and refuse to reconcile when they run into difficulties.

Blaming parents for most estrangement problems is completely illogical. To do this, we must believe that age and experience have nothing to do with developing relationship skills.

In fact, we must believe that younger adults have a more mature understanding of relationships than their elders. And since this problem has developed in the last twenty-five to thirty years, to blame parents, we must believe that children have faced greater responsibilities and parents have shown less interest in their children than those in previous generations.

To determine if that's true, let's go back a hundred years to when most families were large and less affluent. During that time, children often had to miss fun activities to help on the farm or with the family business. Parents had greater expectations of their children, and they had less time to encourage them. They weren't assured of government or family benefits, such as college. Yet, despite these hardships, family estrangement was rare.

For example, my father was born in 1925, when my grandparents were farmers in Kansas. His parents and their six children lived in a one-bedroom farmhouse. They usually had food to eat, but they were too poor to afford normal necessities, and everyone who was old enough helped with the chores. During the Dust Bowl years, they lost their farm and moved to Colorado, where they did without many things that other families considered essential. My grandparents were good people and loving parents, but they didn't have the time or money to dote on their children.

When my father enlisted in the Navy during WWII at age 19, his father took him to the train station and said, "Don't volunteer for anything." He didn't say anything affectionate or meaningful. He didn't even say, "I love you."

My grandfather's behavior would be discredited by today's psychology, with my father seen as a victim of poor parenting. But my dad fondly told this story later in his life, explaining that his dad was expressing his love in the only way he knew how. Sadly, giving parents the benefit of the doubt and thinking the best of them has gone out of style in our culture.

In the past seventy-five years, families have become smaller and more affluent. Parents spend more time with their children, and they're more apt to affirm them due to self-esteem influences. But scrutinizing and criticizing parents has become increasingly common. And popular psychology supports this attitude, helping adult children take on the victim mentality we discussed in previous chapters.

The Most Underestimated Command

On Mother's Day and Father's Day, we typically hear sermons about parents' responsibility to bring their children up in the nurture and admonition of the Lord. We rarely hear about the importance of honoring parents. This has become one of the most ignored and underestimated commands in Scripture. When it's addressed, it's typically only applied to underage children.

This is definitely part of Satan's plan to damage families and deprive them of spiritual blessings. God couldn't have emphasized the importance of this command more thoroughly than He did, making it the first command regarding human relationships in the Ten Commandments: "Honor your father and your mother, so that you may live long in the land the LORD your God is giving you" (Exod. 20:12). Ephesians 6:1–3 confirms the permanence of the command, and a unique element of the command is emphasized. It is "the first commandment with a promise."

In the Old Testament, God commanded the nation of Israel to put to death any children who cursed their parents (Lev. 20:9). This was a civil law for a specific period in Israel's history, not a permanent law. It sounds harsh to us, but it shows the emphasis God put on honor and respect for parents. And God's strong punishment for this sin warns us that cultures characterized by parental dishonor are headed for ruin.

> ***Christ said that anyone who dishonors his or her parents worships God in vain.***

In Matthew 15:1–9, Christ mentioned this Old Testament law, not to reinstate it, but to remind the Pharisees how strongly God condemns disrespect for parents. The Pharisees tried to convince people that giving to the Temple was more important than caring for their parents' needs. And Christ made it clear that we "curse" our parents by neglect as well as by our words. Note the strong emphasis God gave this sin. Christ said that anyone who dishonors his or her parents worships God in vain.

God knows that all parents are imperfect, and some are downright difficult, but He doesn't provide exceptions to His command. We aren't told to honor our parents if they are worthy of honor. Instead, we honor them because God and His commands are worthy of honor.

Proverbs 30:11–13 describes disrespectful children as "those who curse their fathers / and do not bless their mothers; / those who are pure in their own eyes / and yet are not cleansed of their filth; / those whose eyes are ever so haughty, / whose glances are so disdainful." This accurately describes many adults who expect approval, respect, and honor from their parents while judging, neglecting, and marginalizing them.

We also find a strong figurative warning in Proverbs 30:17: "The eye that mocks a father, / that scorns an aged mother, / will be pecked out by the ravens of the valley, / will be eaten by the vultures." This verse uses figurative language to show how serious it is to mistreat our parents (and is another example of a proverb that's not a promise).

The Gospel According to Absalom

Second Samuel 13 tells the story of King David's son, Amnon, raping his half-sister, Tamar. I can understand why this would anger her full-brother, Absalom. But Absalom made a fatal error. He decided to play God. He didn't appeal to his father, King David, and he didn't follow the laws outlined in Scripture. He took matters into his own hands and murdered Amnon.

People sometimes read this passage and blame David because he didn't use his position as king to punish Amnon. But Scripture tells us that Absalom interfered with the legal process by having Tamar go into seclusion and telling her not to report the rape (13:20). Absalom had already decided to murder Amnon (13:32).

We can't know for sure if this is what kept David from holding Amnon accountable, but we know that Absalom was vengeful and chose to disrespect his father David and mock God's laws. Absalom ended up dying in disgrace for his ungodly attempt to discredit David and steal his kingdom (17:14).

Many Christians have taken on the Absalom mindset, thinking it's their place to judge and punish their parents. But that's God's job, not ours.

"Boundaries" Promote Dishonor

As I mentioned, one of the most popular psychological philosophies causing parental estrangement is the concept of setting up "boundaries." This concept began in secular psychology, but a number of authors and teachers have repackaged it for Christians by badly twisting Scripture passages. It encourages us to cut people off (especially parents) if they don't measure up to our desires. In the end, it teaches people to avoid difficulties instead of working through them.

Most of these estrangement-promoting books, articles, and seminars twist out-of-context Scriptures to fit their goals. They also promote exaggerated rhetoric, calling people who are merely annoying "toxic" and difficult situations "unsafe."

Instead of counseling people to be hopeful and patient and return good for evil, the boundaries teachings encourage adult children to lay down the law with their parents, cutting them off or marginalizing them if they don't live up to specific expectations.

Children who treat their parents this way become weak and self-righteous, never maturing in their relationship skills. Instead of learning how to love imperfect parents and show them respect without being manipulated, boundaries teachings encourage people to manipulate their parents by denying them a normal relationship.

Those who promote these teachings reveal a complete lack of biblical knowledge. Books on this topic are often bestsellers because they appeal to our fallen, selfish human nature. Some go so far as to claim that Christ set boundaries in relationships.

However, we are saved because Christ humbled Himself and accepted terrible mistreatment and hatred to save us. He clearly taught that we should also be willing to be despised for His purposes, and one of His purposes is that we honor our parents.

> Whoever wants to be my disciple must deny themselves and take up their cross daily and follow me. For whoever wants to save their life will lose it, but whoever loses their life for me will save it. (Luke 9:23–24)

Only Satan could convince so many adult children to lose the blessings God promises for those who honor their parents. Satan always has been a skillful deceiver, killing, stealing, and destroying relationships (2 Cor. 4:4; John 10:10).

If only people understood how many emotional, spiritual, and even material blessings they forfeit by failing to honor their parents!

The Rekabites

Let me offer what we might call an "extreme" example of honor. In Jeremiah 35, we read about the Rekabites. Their forefathers asked them to never drink wine, never build houses, and never become farmers. Instead, they were to live in tents as nomads.

Drinking wine, building houses, and farming were not sinful according to God's commands. Furthermore, while we are to honor our parents our entire lives, God doesn't expect adults to obey parents in the same way as children do. But the Rekabites obeyed God's fourth commandment beyond what was required.

Our present culture would call the Rekabite parents manipulative, controlling, and unreasonable. Freudian psychology would describe Rekabite children as victims, and boundaries teachings would tell them to end contact with their parents. But God called attention to the Rekabites so Jeremiah would include their exemplary lives in God's divinely inspired Word.

We don't need to take honor to the level of the Rekabites, but we must carefully and prayerfully consider how God judges our relationships with our parents. Our attitudes toward our parents reflect our character and faith (Phil. 2:3–4; John 14:21).

It's Never Too Late

I was in my 40s when I began to understand the emphasis God placed on honoring parents. Even though I had a good relationship with my mom and dad, God began to show me ways to more fully honor them. Thankfully, before they died, I was genuinely learning how to do that.

The first step is forgiveness. Every parent is imperfect and does things that disappoint us. We can forgive them and experience spiritual growth. Or we can harbor bitterness, claim we're victims, and carry out revenge.

I know women who were abused by a parent, yet they've offered more grace to their parents than others who were not abused. They understood Hebrews 12:15, "See to it that no one falls short of the grace of God and that no bitter root grows up to cause trouble and defile many."

> ***No matter what our parents did wrong, they also did some things right.***

The next step is gratitude (1 Thess. 5:18). No matter what our parents did wrong, they also did some things right. If we dwell on the good and let our parents know how much we appreciate what they've done for us, we'll have a type of peace that only God can give (Phil. 4:8).

After forgiveness and gratitude, a variety of things can improve parental relationships, such as staying in regular contact, showing them affection, offering to help when they have needs, using respectful tones and words when speaking to them, and encouraging them to have a close relationship with their grandchildren. And I'd like to add this for those whose parents have already died: Even after a parent has passed away, we can repent of our disrespect and honor their memory.

Self-esteem and boundaries teachings are the types of philosophies Colossians 2:8 warns us against: "See to it that no one takes you captive through hollow and deceptive philosophy, which depends on human tradition and the elemental spiritual forces of this world rather than on Christ."

Therefore, if we seek counseling for any kind of relationship problem, we should find counselors who encourage forgiveness and reconciliation. This doesn't mean we can't be honest about our parents' sins and failures, but that shouldn't be our focus. When we wholeheartedly obey God, we find that His commands are designed for our good.

Honoring a Parent's Request

God does not want children of any age to honor ungodly requests from parents. But what about requests that are not ungodly?

Must adults let their parents make decisions for them? Is that part of honor?

I was married with two adult children when my husband retired from twenty-two years of service in the Army, and we moved temporarily back to my hometown. My father, a retired contractor, felt we should buy a lot so he could help us build a house. I told him we were too unsure of our future to do something that permanent. But he kept insisting.

Then, one day as I was praying, I felt the Lord convict me that I was treating my father's advice as if he were my friend, not my parent. And parental honor should be of a higher standard than respect for friends. So I went to my father, apologized for not taking his advice seriously, and told him that my husband and I would make it a matter of prayer.

We took time to sincerely pray about the situation and felt the Lord leading us not to build a house. When I explained this to my father, I could tell he appreciated the respectful way we'd handled it. He could finally accept our answer.

When we become adults, honoring our parents does not mean doing everything they ask, but it does mean listening and treating their advice with more respect than suggestions we might receive from friends. If our parents don't understand our faith or oppose what God calls us to do, we must put God first. But with God's help we can forgive our parents and continue treating them with respect, kindness, and grace (1 Pet. 3:9; Eph. 4:31–32).

Digging Deeper: Questions for Group or Personal Study

1. It's easy to understand why obeying Ephesians 6:1–3 will make things go well for us. Obedience to God's commands helps us avoid unnecessary consequences. But the promise of long life is harder to understand, because some children who

respect their parents die young and some who dishonor their parents live long lives. Some Bible scholars believe the promise refers to eternal life. Others believe it is a general principle, which means those who honor their parents will avoid foolish sins that would otherwise end their lives early. Check out these passages to better understand this promise: Isaiah 57:1; Hebrews 11; Second Timothy 4:6–8; Philippians 1:20–26. If these passages don't give you the clarity you'd like, remember First Corinthians 13:12.

2. Read Proverbs 1:8, 20:20, 23:22, First Timothy 5:1, and First Peter 5:5. Consider sharing these verses in your small group or Bible study for discussion.

3. How can you apply Philippians 2:3 to your relationship with your parents in practical ways each week?

4. What do Second Timothy 3:1–5 and Romans 1:28–32 tell us about the importance of honoring parents?

5. When we read about the Rekabites in Jeremiah 35:1–6, it might appear that God was tempting them to disobey their father's instructions. How do First Corinthians 10:13 and James 1:2–15 help explain this situation?

6. Self-righteous attitudes are grounded in hypocrisy, and this is reflected in the life of Absalom. Remember that the rape of his sister caused Absalom to murder his brother. Read Second Samuel 16:20–22 and note the irony and hypocrisy in Absalom's evil actions.

7. If you own a "Christian" book on boundaries, you might want to use it in a group study as an example of half-truth methods and identify Scriptures that have been taken out of context or misused.

7

Half-Truth: "God's Love Is Unconditional"

THIS MAY BE the hardest half-truth for most readers to accept because this description of God's love is without a doubt the most popular in our culture. However, many solid Bible teachers have refuted it.[1]

When Christians borrow words from secular culture, we usually make our message more popular but less accurate. And the secular expression "unconditional love" is perhaps the best example. Most Christians see this definition as the highest and most admirable way to explain God's love, when it actually carries meanings that minimize and misrepresent the biblical definition.

While we need to honestly and biblically examine the term "unconditional love," let's start by acknowledging that God's love is so incredible that it's beyond our full understanding:

> I pray that you, being rooted and established in love, may have power, together with all the Lord's holy people, to grasp how wide and long and high and deep is the love of Christ, and to

---

1 For instance: Tim Challies (https://www.challies.com/christian-living/a-jealous-love/); R.C. Sproul (https://learn.ligonier.org/podcasts/ultimately-with-rc-sproul/is-the-love-of-god-unconditional); George Sinclair (https://ca.thegospelcoalition.org/article/good-news-god-not-love-unconditionally/); and Bob Russell (https://bobrussell.org/spiritual-myth-3-god-loves-you-unconditionally/).

know this love that surpasses knowledge—that you may be filled to the measure of all the fullness of God. (Eph. 3:17–19)

God's love "surpasses knowledge" (NIV). It "is too great to understand fully" (NLT). Yet, we must be careful to define it as God defines it in Scripture, neither adding nor subtracting from the biblical explanations. So please start with a teachable spirit and pray for discernment as we answer some common questions regarding the term "unconditional."

Doesn't Scripture Describe God's Love as Unconditional?

No. When describing God's love, the Greek and Hebrew manuscripts of Scripture do not contain any word or combination of words that would accurately translate as "unconditional." And the word is not used to describe God's love in any legitimate translation of the Bible.

> ***The popular explanation of* agápe *is not biblical. It is similar to the English word "love" in that it has a range of meanings based on the context.***

You might think, "What about the Greek word *agápe*?"

When something is said often enough, we assume it's correct, but the popular explanation of *agápe* is not biblical.[2] According to *Strong's Exhaustive Concordance of the Bible,* the word *agápe* means "love, i.e. Affection or benevolence; specially (plural) a love-feast —(feast of) charity(-ably), dear, love."[3]

The word *agápe* is similar to the English word "love" in that it has a range of meanings based on the context. For example, we use the same word to say, "I love hamburgers" or "I love God." And that's true for the Greek word *agápe*. It refers to the shallow love of the tax

2 R.F. Youngblood, F.F. Bruce, and R.K. Harrison, *Nelson's New Illustrated Bible Dictionary* (Thomas Nelson Publishers, 1995), 23.

3 James Strong, *Strong's Exhaustive Concordance of the Bible* (https://biblehub.com/greek/26.htm), accessed June 16, 2025.

collectors in Matthew 5:46, the respectful love for a church leader in First Thessalonians 5:13, or the perfect, sacrificial love of Christ in John 3:16. Yes, the Greek word *agápe* is used in all of those verses.

We should "always be prepared" to explain our faith to others (1 Pet. 3:15), but we should seek to do it honestly and accurately. If we are going to emphasize a point by explaining the meaning of the original Greek word, let's do our homework. Let's quit passing along uneducated misunderstandings and take time to correctly handle God's Word. Let's be like the noble Bereans and make sure Scripture supports what we are taught (Acts 17:11). We must get our definition of God's love from Scripture.

Hasn't God's Love Always Been Described as Unconditional?

No. This is a modern term with an unclear source. Some believe it originated with the agnostic humanistic psychologist Carl Rogers, who taught "unconditional positive regard." Others believe the term became popular through the teachings of Erich Fromm, an atheist humanistic psychologist. But neither of these associated this term with God's love. Whatever its origin, the term wasn't used by Christians until the 20th century.

Doesn't Unconditional Describe the Highest Form of Love?

No. If it did, it would be used in Scripture. To accurately understand God's love we must depend on His divinely inspired Word so our definitions fit what Scripture teaches.

God Loved Us While We Were Yet Sinners (1 John 4:19; Rom. 5:8). Doesn't That Make His Love Unconditional?

No. God loves mankind enough to offer us salvation. But it's not an unconditional offer. His salvation is given only to those who believe.

> If anyone acknowledges that Jesus is the Son of God, God lives in them and they in God. And so we know and rely on the love God has for us. God is love. Whoever lives in love lives in God, and God in them. (1 John 4:15–16)

God Doesn't Stop Loving Us When We Sin. So Doesn't That Make His Love Unconditional?

No. That makes His love forgiving. And the fact that He has to forgive us shows that He sets up conditions for right and wrong.

God's Love Is Not Based on Our Goodness. Doesn't That Make It Unconditional?

No. Our salvation is not based on our goodness, but the *validity* of our salvation is based on the condition that we truly love God and seek to obey Him. Please note the conditional explanation Christ gave in the following verses.

> As the Father has loved me, so have I loved you. Now remain in my love. If you keep my commands, you will remain in my love, just as I have kept my Father's commands and remain in his love. I have told you this so that my joy may be in you and that your joy may be complete. My command is this: Love each other as I have loved you. Greater love has no one than this: to lay down one's life for one's friends. You are my friends if you do what I command. (John 15:9–14)

Aren't God's Promises Given to Us Unconditionally?

No. For example, when God promised never to leave us or forsake us (Rom. 8:38–39), that's a fully trustworthy, unchanging promise. But it's conditional. It only applies to believers. Those who don't believe will one day be eternally separated from God in hell (2 Thess. 1:6–10).

One promise that might be considered unconditional is that the sun rises on both the evil and the good (Matt. 5:44–45), but that is a temporary promise, which only applies on earth. God also promised conditional rewards after we are saved:

> Be careful not to practice your righteousness in front of others to be seen by them. If you do, you will have no reward from your Father in heaven. (6:1)

> But love your enemies, do good to them, and lend to them without expecting to get anything back. Then your reward will be great, and you will be children of the Most High, because he is kind to the ungrateful and wicked. (Luke 6:35)
>
> Serve wholeheartedly, as if you were serving the Lord, not people, because you know that the Lord will reward each one for whatever good they do, whether they are slave or free. (Eph. 6:7–8)

Is Unconditional the Same as Eternal, Perfect, Patient, Holy, and Persevering?

No. Those wonderful adjectives are used in Scripture, along with many other accurate descriptions of God's love. They fit together beautifully to give us a clearer understanding, but none of them means unconditional. Why would we want to use words not found in Scripture when they are misleading—especially when we have so many accurate biblical descriptions?

Why Do We Misunderstand the Word Unconditional?

Most Christians use the term "unconditional love" with good intentions, thinking it expresses God's undeserved grace and favor, which isn't based on good works or perfect behavior. They are not intentionally trying to distort biblical truths, and they're unaware of the many false teachings the term generates. I used it myself before I learned how often it was misapplied. But being biblically accurate should be our highest goal.

What Exactly is Unconditional Love?

Unconditional means "not subject to any conditions." That makes "unconditional love" an oxymoron. Genuine love must be built on honesty, and must have moral values. These are conditions. If an act or feeling lacks these, at best it's neutral, and at worst it's evil.

For example, if a husband truly had no conditions on his love for his wife, he would feel exactly the same about her whether she was faithful or had adulterous affairs. If parents had unconditional love for their children, they would never set rules for their behavior, nor would they punish them, even when doing so was for their best good.

If God had unconditional love, He would see all behaviors as loving, whether sinful or godly. He'd accept us as we are and make no attempt to free us from our sins. And that's exactly what many popular false teachers claim.

So before getting into the many errors produced by the term "unconditional love," let's summarize God's love.

- The greatest act of God's love toward man is conditional, based on our belief. This is clear in the single verse most often used to define our salvation, John 3:16.
- God defines moral behavior and judges men and women based on conditions of right and wrong (3:18–21).
- The reason we need a Savior is because we have fallen short of God's conditions for good and evil (Rom. 3:23).
- The genuineness of our salvation is conditional, judged by our motives (Matt. 7:21–23) and by our obedience (John 14:21).
- The rewards of the Christian life are conditional (Eph. 6:7–8).

God's love is perfect and life-giving because it's based on holiness. If His love were unconditional, we would never know the beauty of His purity and righteousness. Let's discard this human explanation of God's love and use scriptural descriptions.

Why Calling God's Love Unconditional is Dangerous

Trying to disconnect conditions from the overall description of God's love is misleading. It doesn't enhance God's love; it removes its purity, justice, goodness, and glory. And it also redefines God's character because "God is love" (1 John 4:8). No wonder it leads to so many serious errors, false teachings, and heresies.

It Undermines Christ's Death

Christians are saved from the eternal death we deserve because Christ fulfilled a condition of God's love that we could not fulfill. If God's love were unconditional, Christ would not have needed to die.

That's exactly what some people now claim. They teach that the God of unconditional love would never plan or require His Son's sacrifice. Instead, they insist it was an unnecessary event caused by human sin and has nothing to do with our salvation.

Christ's death is clearly described as God's purposeful and necessary plan for our salvation, fulfilling a condition of God's pure and righteous love.

Scripture completely destroys that false teaching: "[Jesus] was handed over to you by God's deliberate plan and foreknowledge; and you, with the help of wicked men, put him to death by nailing him to the cross" (Acts 2:23).

Christ's death is clearly described as God's purposeful and necessary plan for our salvation, fulfilling a condition of God's pure and righteous love. John 10:17–18 explains that Jesus died according to the command of the Father.

Colossians 1:19–20 says, "God was pleased to have all his fullness dwell in him, and through him to reconcile to himself all things, whether things on earth or things in heaven, by making peace through his blood, shed on the cross."

In order to save us, an important condition had to be fulfilled, and Christ, the perfect, sinless Son of God, was the only One who could fulfill it. This message may seem foolish to the unsaved, "but to us who are being saved it is the power of God" (1 Cor. 1:18).

It Denies the Necessity of Belief

Besides misrepresenting the purpose of Christ's death, calling God's love unconditional also misleads unbelievers. It gives the impression that they need not make a decision to follow Christ because He will love them and save them no matter what beliefs they hold.

This would mean that God values God-haters and God-lovers, victims and criminals, godly people and wicked people, atheists and believers alike. If He loved unconditionally, He'd view cults, paganism, Christianity, and satanism the same, and His love would see no difference between an unrepentant serial killer and a Christian martyr.

Sadly, this is the message many people are hearing, and it has greatly advanced the popularity of *universal salvation*, the belief that all people will be saved.

It Downplays Faithful Maturity

Within the body of Christ, the talk about God's unconditional love has led some believers to think God treats all of His children equally—those who serve Him faithfully and those who don't. It's true that God is equally available to all believers, and He is ready to reward those who seek Him with equal rewards. But those who seek Him wholeheartedly receive blessings that people with lazy faith don't receive.

All genuine Christians are working out their salvation, as described in Philippians 2:12–13. Some do so carefully, deliberately, and wholeheartedly, focusing on heavenly treasure and God's purposes (Phil. 3:12–16; Matt. 6:19–21; Eph. 2:10). Other Christians let themselves get sidetracked. They don't live sinful lives, but neither do they seek to serve God wholeheartedly. Paul explains this difference in First Corinthians 3:10–15:

> By the grace God has given me, I laid a foundation as a wise builder, and someone else is building on it. But each one should build with care. For no one can lay any foundation other than the one already laid, which is Jesus Christ. If anyone builds on this foundation using gold, silver, costly stones, wood, hay or straw, their work will be shown for what it is, because the Day will bring it to light. It will be revealed with fire, and the fire

> will test the quality of each person's work. If what has been built survives, the builder will receive a reward. If it is burned up, the builder will suffer loss but yet will be saved—even though only as one escaping through the flames.

No jealousy will exist in heaven, but some people will be rewarded for their faithfulness in ways we don't yet understand. This has nothing to do with salvation, but it has everything to do with how we live out our faith. Will we build with "gold, silver, and costly stones" or "wood, hay, and straw"? It matters to God, and He rewards His followers conditionally, based on their faithfulness to the opportunities He provides in their lives.

Unconditional love also encourages the belief that God sees all sins the same, another half-truth belief we'll discuss in Chapter 8.

It Promotes Antinomianism

A further problem with the belief in equal rewards is related to misunderstandings about condemnation. Romans 8:1–2 says, "Therefore, there is now no condemnation for those who are in Christ Jesus, because through Christ Jesus the law of the Spirit who gives life has set you free from the law of sin and death."

Chapter 4 explained that misunderstandings about condemnation are involved in the "judge not" half-truth, and they also play a part in misunderstandings about God's love. Some people who believe in unconditional love claim that because we're forgiven, we aren't held responsible for our sins during our earthly lives, and nothing we do affects our relationship with the Lord.

This attitude toward sin was also present in the early church. It's called antinomianism and Paul addressed it in Romans 6:

> What shall we say, then? Shall we go on sinning so that grace may increase? By no means! We are those who have died to sin; how can we live in it any longer? . . . Shall we sin because we are not under the law but under grace? By no means! (6:1–2, 15)

The condemnation addressed in Romans 8:1–2 is eternal punishment. Christians will not be punished in hell, but we still suffer consequences for our sins on earth because God disciplines and punishes those He loves (Heb. 12:5–6).

We should take our sins *more* seriously after conversion, not less seriously. The context of Romans 8:1–2 makes this clear. A few verses later, verses 12–13 say, "Therefore, brothers and sisters, we have an obligation—but it is not to the flesh, to live according to it. For if you live according to the flesh, you will die; but if by the Spirit you put to death the misdeeds of the body, you will live."

Paul sets an example of the appropriate Christian attitude toward Christian growth in Philippians 3:10–14:

> I want to know Christ—yes, to know the power of his resurrection and participation in his sufferings, becoming like him in his death, and so, somehow, attaining to the resurrection from the dead.
>
> Not that I have already obtained all this, or have already arrived at my goal, but I press on to take hold of that for which Christ Jesus took hold of me. Brothers and sisters, I do not consider myself yet to have taken hold of it. But one thing I do: Forgetting what is behind and straining toward what is ahead, I press on toward the goal to win the prize for which God has called me heavenward in Christ Jesus.

The term "unconditional love" leads to serious confusion and compromise. It misrepresents the beauty, holiness, justice, and righteousness of God's love and character, and it has contributed to a number of false views about our salvation and our responsibilities as believers. Consider what Scripture teaches, and avoid the confusion and errors this description causes.

Digging Deeper: Questions for Group or Personal Study

1. Why do you think so many Christians insist on using a word that is not found in Scripture, a word that causes these serious misunderstandings? Does First Corinthians 2 help you answer this question?

2. Read and meditate on Psalm 103. It expresses some of the many benefits of God's wonderful love. In verses 11–18 it explains who receives those benefits.

3. The idea of unconditional love has caused some believers to assume that we will face no final judgment. If we take John 5:24 out of context, we might believe this as well, but let's add it to Second Corinthians 5:10 and First Corinthians 3:10–15. What do you conclude from these passages?

4. How does church discipline contradict the concept of unconditional love? (Read Matthew 18:15–17 and First Corinthians 5.)

5. Consider these passages in regard to the term unconditional love: Psalm 5:4–6; Proverbs 6:16–19; Matthew 7:21–23; 18:21–35; Second Timothy 2:19.

6. When you read the Bible, why not keep a list of the different ways it describes God's love? This can help you accurately understand His awesome character.

8

Half-Truth: "Evangelism Should Avoid Hard Truths"

ANOTHER RESULT of exalting man is the view that we can only win souls if we avoid the "hard truths" in Scripture. But whenever we focus on making people feel comfortable, we offer a half-truth gospel based on empty, humanistic love.

Don't Talk About Sin or Hell

When people believe that God's love is unconditional, they think evangelism should focus on making people feel loved, approved, and accepted. But we can't share the gospel message without talking about sin and hell.

If we don't first hear and understand the bad news, we can't understand the good news. When we recognize that our sins have separated us from our holy God and made us fully deserve hell, we are ready to appreciate and cherish the news that if we trust Christ, His sacrifice brings us complete forgiveness and salvation.

If you have any doubt that this is the message we are called to proclaim, look to Christ's example. From the start of His ministry, "Jesus began to preach, 'Repent, for the kingdom of heaven has come near' " (Matt. 4:17). He denounced the locations where people had seen His signs and wonders but refused to repent (11:20–21).

Jesus clearly explained, "I have not come to call the righteous, but sinners to repentance" (Luke 5:32). He warned people that if they didn't repent, they would perish (13:3, 5). And He told His disciples that they were called to preach "repentance for the forgiveness of sins" (24:47).

The gospel is not: "Feel good about yourself because God loves you." The gospel is: "Realize your sin separates you from God, but He lovingly offers you forgiveness and eternal life if you repent, believe, and follow."

Do you remember the first time you understood the gospel message, the first time you realized the greatest act of love in your life was Christ dying for your sins? The true gospel makes us sad before it makes us happy, but it brings incredible joy and comfort!

Ashamed of God's Wrath

When we see God's love as unconditional, we misunderstand the serious nature of our sin, the importance of justice, and the incredible mercy of God. And this makes us uncomfortable with God's wrath. That's why it's become popular to claim, "God doesn't send anyone to hell. They send themselves."

Yes, people choose to reject Christ, but they wouldn't and couldn't, throw themselves into hell any more than we can send ourselves to heaven. God's infinite wisdom is based on pure and holy moral truths. He alone has a right to send people to hell, and we shouldn't be ashamed to admit it.

We would never say that a serial killer executed himself, or that a thief put himself in prison. The behavior caused the person's execution or imprisonment, but the judicial system punished the person. Why then do we feel that we need to somehow excuse God's right to send people to hell?

I think it goes back to our fear of presenting God as holy and just, even though both are important qualities of love. We've come to see punishment as hateful, and that's why so many Christians refuse correction. When we come to Christ, "He does not treat us as our sins deserve / or repay us according to our iniquities" (Ps. 103:10). But if we refuse to turn to Him, He *does* treat us as our sins deserve and *does* repay us according to our iniquities.

> ***The Bible doesn't sugarcoat the gospel, nor should we. We should never be ashamed to explain God's right to judge and punish.***

Let's reject this popular movement that presents the good news without presenting the bad news. The Bible doesn't sugarcoat the gospel, nor should we:

> The wrath of God is being revealed from heaven against all the godlessness and wickedness of people, who suppress the truth by their wickedness, since what may be known about God is plain to them, because God has made it plain to them. For since the creation of the world God's invisible qualities—his eternal power and divine nature—have been clearly seen, being understood from what has been made, so that people are without excuse. (Rom. 1:18–20)

The two verses immediately before this passage about God's wrath clearly show that we should never be ashamed to explain God's right to judge and punish:

> For I am not ashamed of the gospel, because it is the power of God that brings salvation to everyone who believes: first to the Jew, then to the Gentile. For in the gospel the righteousness of God is revealed—a righteousness that is by faith from first to last, just as it is written: "The righteous will live by faith." (1:16–17)

If we believe the gospel brings salvation and is based on righteousness, we will not be ashamed to share it honestly and fully.

The Words of Jesus

Our culture typically presents Jesus as a softspoken, non-confrontational buddy, but that's not the Jesus of the Bible. The true Jesus who came to save us from our sins talked quite boldly about hell:

> But I tell you that anyone who is angry with a brother or sister will be subject to judgment. Again, anyone who says to a brother or sister, "Raca," is answerable to the court. And anyone who says, "You fool!" will be in danger of the fire of hell. (Matt. 5:22)
>
> If your right eye causes you to stumble, gouge it out and throw it away. It is better for you to lose one part of your body than for your whole body to be thrown into hell. (5:29)
>
> Enter through the narrow gate. For wide is the gate and broad is the road that leads to destruction, and many enter through it. (7:13)
>
> Do not be afraid of those who kill the body but cannot kill the soul. Rather, be afraid of the One who can destroy both soul and body in hell. (10:28)
>
> What good will it be for someone to gain the whole world, yet forfeit their soul? Or what can anyone give in exchange for their soul? For the Son of Man is going to come in his Father's glory with his angels, and then he will reward each person according to what they have done. (16:26–27)
>
> You snakes! You brood of vipers! How will you escape being condemned to hell? Therefore I am sending you prophets and sages and teachers. Some of them you will kill and crucify; others you will flog in your synagogues and pursue from town to town. (23:33–34)

In Matthew 25, Christ used three parables to highlight eternal rewards and punishments, and He warned that those who rejected Him would be thrown "into the darkness, where there will be weeping and gnashing of teeth" (25:30).

Christ's warning in Luke 12:4–5 was also strong and clear: "I tell you, my friends, do not be afraid of those who kill the body and after that can do no more. But I will show you whom you should fear: Fear him who, after your body has been killed, has authority to throw you into hell. Yes, I tell you, fear him."

Four Hard Questions About Hell

Because hell is part of the gospel message, we should be prepared for these four questions that may arise when we share Christ.

1. Why Would a Loving God Send People to Hell?

As we've already discussed, genuine love has certain conditions of goodness and holiness. For example, a loving husband doesn't beat his wife, and a loving parent protects a child from molestation. Genuine love is offended by evil and acts against it. "Love must be sincere. Hate what is evil; cling to what is good" (Rom. 12:9).

We are made in God's image, and we should be the first to understand why God is offended by those who reject His loving offer of salvation. He's not unfair. He gives us a choice. From the beginning, God has made this clear.

When Cain harbored sinful thoughts toward Abel, God intervened: "Then the LORD said to Cain, 'Why are you angry? Why is your face downcast? If you do what is right, will you not be accepted? But if you do not do what is right, sin is crouching at your door; it desires to have you, but you must rule over it' " (Gen. 4:6–7).

Of course, Cain, like most of the world, chose sin and paid the price. But it was his choice.

Those who reject Christ do so "without excuse" because "since the creation of the world God's invisible qualities—his eternal power and divine nature—have been clearly seen, being understood from what has been made" (Rom. 1:20).

In addition, God gives everyone a conscience, writing His law on their hearts (2:12–16). He promises that all who seek

Him will find Him (Jer. 29:13; Luke 11:9–13); those who refuse to seek Him do so because they love darkness instead of light (John 3:19).

God wants men and women to choose redemption and heaven (1 Tim. 2:3–6), but He won't force people to love Him, and He won't let unrepentant sin infect eternity (Rev. 21). Even if we don't fully understand the concept of hell, we can trust God's just and loving character (Jer. 9:23–24).

2. Why Did God Put the Forbidden Tree in the Garden of Eden?

We don't hear this question as often as the first, but it's important to know how to answer it. God tests our faith, but He never tempts anyone (James 1:12–15). And whenever we are tempted, God gives us a "way out" (1 Cor. 10:13).

Sin is always a choice—a choice no one forces us to make. And let's step back and think about this situation realistically. God gave Adam and Eve one rule—just one (Gen. 2:16–17). They had a plethora of choices for delicious, nutritious fruit (2:8–9). Only one fruit was forbidden—just one.

God created Adam and Eve "very good" (1:31). They could have chosen not to sin. They had regular fellowship with God and didn't have the insecurities, concerns, or fears of our fallen human nature. Despite all of these blessings, Adam and Eve chose to sin and break the one rule God had given them.

> ***My sadness over Adam's sin is only exceeded by my awe of God's incredible love.***

But this is the part that really blows my mind, that turns my sadness into incredible joy and gratitude: God didn't destroy them! In Genesis 3:15, on the field of their defeat, He gave them (and us) a clue about our coming Redeemer. My sadness over Adam's sin is only exceeded by my awe of God's incredible love.

3. Why Did God Create Adam and Eve with the Ability to Sin?

God can do anything He wants. He could have programmed us like robots, dictating our every move. But He didn't want robots. He wanted us to understand genuine love, and genuine love requires freedom to choose.

Would you want your husband and children to be "programmed" to love you whether they wanted to or not? We don't want that because we're made in God's image, and He doesn't want to force us to love Him either.

So God created Adam and Eve and all of humanity with the ability to make choices. Even though He wants us to make the right choices, He doesn't force us to do that. This answer should satisfy us, but we also must admit that we can't fully understand every aspect of God's plans because God's ways are beyond our full understanding (Isa. 55:9).

4. Why Are We Punished for Adam's Sin?

We might hear this question from unbelievers, but it's also relevant for believers who simply want to better understand the gospel. We cannot fully comprehend all aspects of this question, but let's look at what Scripture teaches us in this area.

Why was the whole human race condemned for Adam's sin? Why do we come into the world with a fallen human nature and automatically have to deal with sin, sickness, death, and decay when we didn't eat the forbidden fruit?

This happens because Adam was our representative (Rom. 5:12–15). Although the Bible doesn't specifically say it, I believe we'd have done exactly what Adam and Eve did, if we had been in their places.

It's hard to fully understand this concept, but we can trust God because He is a God "who exercises kindness, justice and righteousness on earth." In fact, He delights in those things (Jer. 9:24).

And we need to keep in mind that only once did God punish an innocent man: Jesus "was pierced for our transgressions, / he was crushed for our iniquities; / the punishment that brought us peace was upon him, / and by his wounds we are healed" (Isa. 53:5).

The good news continues because "Just as we are now like the earthly man, we will someday be like the heavenly man" (1 Cor. 15:45–49, NLT).

When I became a Christian, I wanted to know all of the specifics. I didn't want to have a single unanswered question about God. But I soon found that my finite human mind would never fully understand the infinite mind of God. And that gave me joy to know that His wisdom was beyond human wisdom. The important thing to understand was that I could trust His goodness.

At that point, one of my favorite verses became First Corinthians 13:12: "For now we see only a reflection as in a mirror; then we shall see face to face. Now I know in part; then I shall know fully, even as I am fully known."

He Gives Us All We Need

> His divine power has given us everything we need for a godly life through our knowledge of him who called us by his own glory and goodness. (2 Pet. 1:3)

We cannot fully understand every detail about our magnificent, infinite God, but His divinely inspired Word gives us everything we need to understand our salvation and to share His truth with others. So let's share it accurately. Let's tell people the bad news as well as the good news, the strong and firm gospel message, not a limp replacement.

Digging Deeper: Questions for Group or Personal Study

1. We have looked at passages in which Christ spoke about hell. Look up several additional passages from the New Testament, such as Second Thessalonians 1:5–9; Second Peter 2:4–9; Revelation 14:11. How do these verses further expand your understanding of hell?

2. Eve was the first human to sin, and she tempted Adam to join her. Eve was held responsible for her sin, but Adam was held responsible for bringing sin into the world (Rom. 5:12–19; 1 Cor. 15:21–22). Read Genesis 3:17–19, First Timothy 2:13–14, and Ephesians 5:23. How do these passages help us better understand why Adam was held responsible?

3. At times in history, most men and women felt unworthy of God's love and salvation. Do you think that attitude is prevalent today?

4. What insights about hell can we gain from Matthew 13:36–43 and the story of Lazarus and the rich man in Luke 16:19–31?

5. Think through how to share the gospel with a non-Christian friend, sharing both the bad news and the good news. Consider ways to make the presentation more personal by sharing aspects of your own salvation and passages of Scripture that helped you understand the gospel.

9

Half-Truth: "God Will Save Everyone"

WE'VE MENTIONED universal salvation, but let's discuss it in more detail. Non-Christians from various backgrounds have long held universalist beliefs, claiming that all people will pass from life into eternal paradise, no matter what they believe. And when it became popular to define God's love as unconditional, an increasing number of professing Christians adopted the modified version of universalism, which is called "universal salvation."

Maintaining the belief that Christ is the only way to be saved, universal salvation claims that each person will be reconciled to Christ after death and enter heaven with those who believed in Christ on earth.

Good Judge, Bad Judge: Why Universal Salvation Mocks Grace and Justice

To better understand universal salvation, consider the scenario of a serial killer who is brought before a judge with undeniable evidence that he mercilessly murdered a number of people, and on facing the judge, he shows no remorse.

Judge #1 hears the case, examines the evidence, verifies the man's guilt, and gives him life in prison or the death penalty.

Judge #2 hears the case, examines the evidence, verifies the man's guilt, and frees him—giving him every privilege that a law-abiding citizen would have. Which is the good judge?

Judge #2 represents the Jesus of universal salvation—a Jesus who unconditionally saves everyone. Despite the fact that God gives us an opportunity to repent and be saved on earth, universalists believe God should reward those who refuse. This makes the Bible a book of lies, but some professing Christians insist it's feasible.

But let's talk about Judge #1. He is similar to the real Jesus, but the real Jesus is dealing with eternal reward and punishment, not simply earthly consequences for sin. He declares the man guilty and sentences him to hell.

But He doesn't stop there. He offers the serial killer a complete pardon if he sincerely repents and puts his trust in Christ before his earthly death. He can do this because Christ bore the punishment for this man's sin on the cross (1 Pet. 2:24).

Christ promises this serial killer, and sinners like you and me, that we may have earthly consequences, but we can be eternally pardoned and blessed if we believe in Him. But those who promote universal salvation believe this isn't enough. They insist that Christ should reward the serial killer, even if he never repents or believes. In fact, they say God isn't a good God if He doesn't pardon everyone, no matter what they believe or how they've lived.

The bottom line of universal salvation is the belief that nothing we do makes us *unworthy* of heaven. The bottom line of biblical Christianity is the belief that nothing we do makes us *worthy* of heaven (Rom. 3:12, 23; Gal. 6:7).

We accept Christ's offer of salvation before we die, not afterwards: "Just as each person is destined to die once and after that comes judgment, so also Christ was offered once for all time as a sacrifice to take away the sins of many people. He will come again, not to deal with our sins, but to bring salvation to all who are eagerly waiting for him" (Heb. 9:27–28, NLT). This passage not only refutes universal salvation, it refutes reincarnation.

John 3:18 further confirms the reason why some will be condemned and some will be saved: "Whoever believes in [Jesus] is not condemned, but whoever does not believe stands condemned already because they have not believed in the name of God's one and only Son."

> ***We shouldn't be shocked by God's wrath against those who reject Him. We should be shocked by His undeserved forgiveness for us who repent.***

God's wrath is both loving and necessary because punishment is an essential element of justice. It's holy anger: pure, unbiased, just, righteous, and fully deserved. God alone understands every detail of every life perfectly, without misunderstandings, confusion, or false evidence. I don't deserve God's grace, nor do you. We shouldn't be shocked by God's wrath against those who reject Him. We should be shocked by His undeserved forgiveness for us who repent. And lest we think God's wrath is an Old Testament concept, and not part of the New Covenant, we can adjust our thinking by reading the passages below:

> The wrath of God is being revealed from heaven against all the godlessness and wickedness of people, who suppress the truth by their wickedness. (Rom. 1:18)
>
> But because of your stubbornness and your unrepentant heart, you are storing up wrath against yourself for the day of God's wrath, when his righteous judgment will be revealed. (2:5)
>
> Since we have now been justified by his blood, how much more shall we be saved from God's wrath through him! (5:9)
>
> Do not take revenge, my dear friends, but leave room for God's wrath, for it is written: "It is mine to avenge; I will repay," says the Lord. (12:19)

> All of us also lived among them at one time, gratifying the cravings of our flesh and following its desires and thoughts. Like the rest, we were by nature deserving of wrath. (Eph. 2:3)
>
> For of this you can be sure: No immoral, impure or greedy person—such a person is an idolater—has any inheritance in the kingdom of Christ and of God. Let no one deceive you with empty words, for because of such things God's wrath comes on those who are disobedient. (5:5–6)
>
> Put to death, therefore, whatever belongs to your earthly nature: sexual immorality, impurity, lust, evil desires and greed, which is idolatry. Because of these, the wrath of God is coming. (Col. 3:5–6)
>
> God is just: He will pay back trouble to those who trouble you and give relief to you who are troubled, and to us as well. This will happen when the Lord Jesus is revealed from heaven in blazing fire with his powerful angels. He will punish those who do not know God and do not obey the gospel of our Lord Jesus. They will be punished with everlasting destruction and shut out from the presence of the Lord and from the glory of his might on the day he comes to be glorified in his holy people and to be marveled at among all those who have believed. This includes you, because you believed our testimony to you. (2 Thess. 1:6–10)

If we can't trust what God's Word says about punishment, how can we trust what it says about forgiveness?

As Christians, our heart's desire should be to share Christ so men and women can come to a knowledge of the truth. Part of what compels us to share Christ is our belief that those who reject Christ will go to hell. If we care about the eternity of unsaved men and women, we will not deceive them by claiming there is no hell.

Half-truth Argument: Garbage Dumps

In multiple passages when Christ warns of hell, He uses the Greek word *gehenna* (γεέννη). This is the name of a place in the Valley of Hinnom, south of Jerusalem, that contained a large burning garbage dump.

During Old Testament times, it was a place of pagan worship where innocent children were sacrificed to the evil god Molech. In Jeremiah 7:30–33, the Lord said these evil people would be slaughtered in the same place where they sacrificed their children. In Jewish literature, the word became synonymous with a place of divine punishment.

Despite these truths, which help us understand why Christ used this word to symbolize hell, universalists insist it means earthly punishment, not eternal punishment. So let's look at that claim.

First, let's examine the passages that contain the word *gehenna* [γεέννη] and note the context (Matt. 5:22, 29, 30; 10:28; 18:9; 23:15, 33; Mark 9:43, 45, 47; Luke 12:5; James 3:6). In each case, it could logically refer to hell. And Matthew 10:28 clearly refers to more than earthly punishment when Jesus uses *gehenna* and says, "Do not be afraid of those who kill the body but cannot kill the soul. Rather, be afraid of the One who can destroy both soul and body in hell [*gehenna*]."

Next, let's look at Scriptures referring to hell that don't use the word *gehenna.* Revelation 20:15 clearly refers to an end-of-life judgment: "Anyone whose name was not found written in the book of life was thrown into the lake of fire."

Second Thessalonians 1:9 says, "They will be punished with everlasting destruction and shut out from the presence of the Lord and from the glory of His might." Matthew 25:41, 46 and Jude 1:7 also warn of eternal punishment. The passages using *gehenna* don't contradict this truth, they support it. Scripture is clear that unsaved people will go to hell when they die.

Half-truth Argument: God's Desires

Using the verses below, people justify universal salvation by explaining that God's desires will not be thwarted. They insist that since God wants all people to be saved, nothing will stop that from happening.

> This is good, and pleases God our Savior, who wants all people to be saved and to come to a knowledge of the truth. (1 Tim. 2:3–4)

> The Lord is not slow in keeping his promise, as some understand slowness. Instead he is patient with you, not wanting anyone to perish, but everyone to come to repentance. (2 Pet. 3:9)

This argument is illogical. How can anyone look at the prevalence of evil throughout history and think God's desires are never thwarted? Scripture also reveals this truth, clarifying that God's desires are not the same as His decrees.

Genesis begins with Adam and Eve disobeying God's command, and a few chapters later, we find that the human race became so evil that God regretted making them and "his heart was deeply troubled" (Gen. 6:5–6).

Throughout the Old Testament, people grieved God's heart (Ps. 78). And Christians disappoint God if we quench His Spirit (1 Thess. 5:19; Eph. 4:30). God's desires are often unfulfilled, but His purposes will prevail; and He has purposed to reward the repentant with eternal life and punish the wicked in hell.

Half-truth Argument: Everyone!

Romans 11:32 says, "For God has bound all men over to disobedience so that he may have mercy on them all." If we take this verse out of context, it might make us think that everyone will be saved. But Romans 11 explains that both Jews and Gentiles are offered God's mercy; it does not say they are promised salvation. We know this by reading previous verses in the same chapter:

> Consider therefore the kindness and sternness of God: sternness to those who fell, but kindness to you, provided that you continue in his kindness. Otherwise, you also will be cut off. And if they do not persist in unbelief, they will be grafted in, for God is able to graft them in again. (Rom. 11:22–23)

First Corinthians 15:22 is another passage used to claim all will be saved: "For as in Adam all die, so in Christ all will be made alive." Bible scholars offer two explanations. Some say the "all" refers only to those "in Christ." But because the two phrases are equally worded, the more legitimate explanation involves the truth that all are made alive in Christ, but not all are destined for heaven.

Some will rise to be sent to heaven, and others will rise to be sent to hell, as explained in John 5:28–29: "Do not be amazed at this, for a time is coming when all who are in their graves will hear his voice and come out—those who have done what is good will rise to live, and those who have done what is evil will rise to be condemned."

Another passage used to claim that Christ will save everyone is First Timothy 4:10: "We have put our hope in the living God, who is the Savior of all people, and especially of those who believe."

This passage, rather than preaching universal salvation, tells us that Christ is the *potential* Savior of all men and the *actual* Savior of those who believe. He is the only path to salvation; no other way exists.

A Matter of Choice

The claims of universal salvation are typical of half-truth teachings. We can't understand a novel if we only read every other chapter, and we can't bake a cake if we leave out half of the ingredients. We can't understand a biblical principle unless we learn all the Bible teaches on that principle. None of the passages we've discussed contradict each other. Instead, they beautifully combine to give us complete truth.

Jesus warned people of the reality of hell, and we must do the same. Christ's final instructions on earth were for believers to make disciples, teaching others everything He taught, and that includes His strong warnings about hell (Matt. 28:16–20).

In the first book of the Bible, God made it clear that sin is a choice (Gen. 4:6–7). Like Cain, people can choose to let sin rule over them, or they can choose to do what is right. Some of these passages misused by universal salvation teachings show us how much God longs for us to repent and be saved. How can we look on the suffering of Christ and expect Him to save those who reject, ignore, or mock Him their whole lives on earth?

How can we believe He owes us more than what He offers? Our wonderful Lord will not populate heaven with people who've rejected Him here on earth, and I'm grateful for that. Aren't you?

Digging Deeper: Questions for Group or Personal Study

1. If someone told you that universal salvation is loving and only an evil God would create hell, how would you respond? It's good to prepare for questions like these (1 Pet. 3:15–16).

2. The rising of both the saved and unsaved is not only explained in John 5:28–29 (quoted previously), but also in Daniel 12:2 and Acts 24:15. Is this concept new to you?

3. How does Matthew 7:13–14 address the belief that "all roads lead to heaven"? Why do you think that so many people believe that contradictory views of God and salvation can lead to the same end?

4. What desires and attitudes draw people to a belief in universal salvation? Do you think genuine Christians can hold this belief?

5. If we take Romans 2:12–16 out of context, we might conclude that the Jews' final judgment is based on Old Testament law, and the Gentiles' final judgment is based on their conscience. But this passage actually confirms that Jew and Gentile will be on equal footing at the judgment, both falling short of salvation without Christ. Read and ponder these other passages about the final judgment: Matthew 13:24–29, 36–43; 25:31–46; John 5:24–30; Second Corinthians 5:6–10; Hebrews 9:24–27; Revelation 20:11–15.

10

Half-Truth: "All Sins Are the Same in God's Eyes"

MY HUSBAND WAS a career soldier. In the early 1980s, we lived at Ft. Leavenworth, Kansas, where he attended the Command and General Staff College. Ft. Leavenworth is also the location of the military prison, and that's why we met "Bob." He was out of prison appealing a rape charge, and he'd successfully convinced several local Christian leaders that he was a genuine believer who had been falsely accused.

These leaders encouraged Bob to attend our small neighborhood Bible study. After we'd fellowshipped with him for several weeks, we heard he was back in prison. He'd been arrested for raping a local woman, and he was clearly guilty.

When our Bible study met a few days later, we expressed shock and confusion regarding the behavior of this man who had sat in our midst one week earlier. One woman in our group said something Christians often say when they want to sound fair-minded and forgiving: "Well, I know he sinned, but when I gossip, I am no different. God sees all sins the same."

This wasn't the first time I'd heard this statement, but the severity of Bob's sin challenged me to research Scripture. And I found that in two ways, this statement is correct: Any sin, no matter how small, keeps us from heaven if we don't trust Jesus (1 John 1:8–10). And when we repent and believe, God forgives any sin, except blasphemy against the Holy Spirit (Mark 3:28–29). But that is where the equality of sins ends. Scripture explains that God sees sins differently in some important ways.

Motives, Intentions, Knowledge, and Opportunity

The Old Testament laws treated unintentional sins more leniently than deliberate acts of rebellion (e.g., Num. 15:22–31). Murderers were executed, but God established cities of refuge where people could flee to safety if they accidentally killed someone (Deut. 19:1–13).

Similarly, the New Testament explains that God judges sins according to the knowledge and opportunity of those who commit them. In John 19:11, Jesus told Pilate, "You would have no power over me if it were not given to you from above. Therefore, the one who handed me over to you is guilty of a greater sin."

This verse expresses several important truths. God gave Pilate power to rule at this time in history when Jesus would be crucified (Rom. 13:1). But Pilate did not understand the spiritual aspects involved. Judas, who had repeatedly heard Christ's message, and the religious leaders, who had the advantage of knowing Old Testament prophesies about Christ, were guilty of greater sin. Judas and the Jewish leaders were motivated by evil intentions, while Pilate was simply doing his job.

God judges our actions similarly. We know He expects more from an adult than a child and more from a person raised in the nurture of the Lord than a person newly introduced to Christ.

> The servant who knows the master's will and does not get ready or does not do what the master wants will be beaten with many blows. But the one who does not know and does things deserving punishment will be beaten with few blows. From everyone who has been given much, much will be demanded; and from the one who has been entrusted with much, much more will be asked. (Luke 12:47–48)

Modern law mimics these Old and New Testament principles. For example, based on the murderer's intentions, first-degree murder is punished more severely than manslaughter. And people possessing stolen goods will have those goods confiscated, but if they knew the goods were stolen, they'll face criminal charges.

Position and Influence

Position and influence are closely related to knowledge and opportunity with some additional considerations. God judges Christians more strictly according to the impact and authority they have in the body of Christ.

Pastors, teachers, Bible study leaders, or Christians in positions of influence should never take their roles lightly. If they make sinful choices, they have greater power to deceive people, and they can do greater damage to the reputation of the body of Christ. This is explained in James 3:1: "Not many of you should become teachers, my fellow believers, because you know that we who teach will be judged more strictly."

God also considers sins against His children worse than other sins. I used to read Matthew 18:6 and assume that God is especially offended by people who abuse innocent children:

> If anyone causes one of these little ones—those who believe in me—to stumble, it would be better for them to have a large millstone hung around their neck and to be drowned in the depths of the sea.

God certainly considers sins against innocent children to be terrible crimes, but according to Bible scholars, that's not the message of Matthew 18:6. In this verse, Jesus is talking about anyone harming His true children—we who have committed our lives to Him.

If someone causes us to stumble in our faith with false teachings, compromise, or evil influences, God is greatly offended because He loves us deeply: "See what great love the Father has lavished on us, that we should be called children of God! And that is what we are! The reason the world does not know us is that it did not know him" (1 John 3:1).

Types of Sins

God also describes some types of sins as more serious than others. In the Old Testament, some sins only required restitution (e.g., Exod. 22:1–6), but others required the death penalty (e.g., 21:12). Human sacrifice and sexual sins received the highest punishments because they not only damaged the souls of those who committed them, but they also damaged the culture at large (Lev. 18:24–30).

Even though these Old Testament laws were not meant to be enforced during New Testament times, they reveal timeless principles. And we need to recognize the emphasis God placed on sexual sin in both the Old and New Testaments.

> Do you not know that your bodies are members of Christ himself? Shall I then take the members of Christ and unite them with a prostitute? Never! Do you not know that he who unites himself with a prostitute is one with her in body? For it is said, "The two will become one flesh." But whoever is united with the Lord is one with him in spirit.
>
> Flee from sexual immorality. All other sins a person commits are outside the body, but whoever sins sexually sins against their own body. Do you not know that your bodies are temples of the Holy Spirit, who is in you, whom you have received from God? You are not your own; you were bought at a price. Therefore honor God with your bodies. (1 Cor. 6:15–20)

> ***Satan's goal is "to steal and kill and destroy" (John 10:10). His modus operandi is to blind people to the serious consequences of their sins.***

Sexual sins affect us in ways other sins do not. While they can cause physical harm, that's not what sets them apart. Sexual sins deeply involve our whole being: body, soul, and spirit. For the

Christian, this means deliberately dishonoring Christ in a way not replicated in other sins.

This helps us understand why Satan so highly promotes sexual sins. His goal is "to steal and kill and destroy" (John 10:10). His *modus operandi* is to blind people to the serious consequences of their sins (2 Cor. 4:4). He promotes these sins because he wants to mock God's loving commands and bring the greatest harm possible to individuals, families, communities, and nations.

God's View of Sin

Romans 1:18–21 explains that the evidence of God and His design is present in nature, so those who reject God are "without excuse." And Romans 2:15 tells us that all people, even unbelievers, have some understanding of God's laws written on their hearts.

Pastors and teachers who underestimate or approve serious sins are described in Romans 1:32: "Although they know God's righteous decree that those who do such things deserve death, they not only continue to do these very things but also approve of those who practice them."

In First Corinthians 5:6, Paul explained that just as "a little yeast leavens the whole batch of dough," ignoring or offering approval to church members who live sinful lifestyles affects the entire church.

Any sin—great or small—condemns us if we don't trust Christ. Likewise, any sin—great or small—is forgiven when we trust in Christ. However, if we think God looks at childish irresponsibility or gossip on the same level as abortion, murder, or sexual perversion, we do not understand God's character.

Digging Deeper: Questions for Group or Personal Study

1. In Chapter 5, we discussed Moses' humility and dependence on God. However, Moses disobeyed God at the waters of Meribah Kadesh, and God gave him a serious punishment (Num. 20:1–13; Deut. 32:48–52). What principle discussed in the section "***Position and Influence***" helps explain this strong punishment against an otherwise faithful leader?

2. Some scholars believe the unpardonable sin was unique to the Pharisees who witnessed Christ's signs and wonders and attributed them to Satan (Matt. 12:22–24, 31; Mark 3:29; Luke 12:10). They believe this is a sin that can't be committed today. Others believe it is the sin described in Hebrews 6:4–8, in which someone fully understands the gospel but rejects it permanently. How would you respond to someone who came to you distraught because they felt they'd committed the unpardonable sin?

3. Several Scripture passages suggest that hell may have different levels of punishment (e.g. Mark 12:40; 2 Pet. 2:17; Jude 1:13). How does the topic of this chapter address this?

4. Read Numbers 22–24, noting that Balaam hesitantly agreed to do the right thing after God spoke directly to him. But later in his life, Balaam apparently harmed God's people through pagan temptations. Why do you think Balaam's sins are specifically mentioned in Second Peter 2, Jude 1:11, and Revelation 2:12–17?

11

Half-Truth: "Good Christians Enjoy Health and Wealth"

AS A NEW CHRISTIAN, I heard teachings that assured me I'd be healed of any disease and financially blessed in my new faith. But I quickly realized that Scripture—and life—didn't support these beliefs. Even if you haven't been influenced by the health and wealth teachings, it's important to study them so you can help others understand why they are not biblical.

Old Testament Promises

The Old Testament is the divinely inspired Word of God, and it's essential in understanding the mission of Christ. But how do we handle passages that promise health and wealth?

First, we must understand that the Old Testament is the beginning of our story, not the end. It's the true story of creation and the fall of humankind, which brought sin, sickness, poverty, death, and decay into our world. The Old Testament is the true story of God preparing His people for the coming Savior.

We previously discussed how some Old Testament laws and promises were specifically given to the nation of Israel at particular points in history. Some promises were related to the sacrificial, dietary, ceremonial, and cleansing laws that Christ fulfilled. And some of the commands and promises were permanent.

Besides understanding these differences, we need to recognize the different genres in Scripture. For example, as we discussed in Chapter 6, if we overlook Proverbs 1:1–6, we might think that Proverbs is a book of promises, when it is actually a divinely inspired collection of wise sayings.

Proverbs 10:22 might sound like a promise for wealth: "The blessing of the LORD brings wealth, / without painful toil for it." But Proverbs 15:16 says: "Better a little with the fear of the LORD / than great wealth with turmoil."

> ***If we love the Lord and follow His commands, we can avoid some unnecessary financial problems. But our faith gives us contentment in humble circumstances as well.***

Both proverbs contain wisdom. If we love the Lord and follow His commands, we can avoid some unnecessary financial problems. But our faith gives us contentment in humble circumstances as well, a truth further confirmed in Philippians 4:12–13.

Detailed theological explanations exist for determining which laws and which promises apply to New Testament Christians, but the easiest way to differentiate is this: If an Old Testament promise is restated as a promise in the New Testament, it applies to us today.

Jeremiah 29:11 Confusion

Jeremiah 29:11 is a popular example of an Old Testament promise that has application for New Testament believers, but not in the way it is typically presented. This verse is often used to claim that God promises a healthy, wealthy, and unhindered life for His followers.

> "For I know the plans I have for you," declares the LORD, "plans to prosper you and not to harm you, plans to give you hope and a future."

"Plans to prosper" may seem like a promise for wealth, but that's not what the context implies. This promise was given to the Jewish exiles in Babylon, telling them to make the best of their situation because God had good plans for them during and after their captivity.

That captivity lasted seventy years, and many of God's people did not live to see it end. God wasn't assuring them that everything would be easy, nor was He promising them health and wealth. He was assuring them that He would use their captivity for good purposes in their lives. We can apply that promise to our lives because it's restated in a general sense in Romans 8:28.

It's a fitting promise for every Christian to make the most of whatever opportunities God gives us, trusting that He will bring good from every situation—even financial difficulties and health problems—if we seek His will and purposes.

Warnings Against Wealth

The belief that God promises us wealth is easily corrected in Scripture. Jesus didn't encourage us to seek wealth, nor did He promise it. Instead, He said, "Watch out! Be on your guard against all kinds of greed; life does not consist in an abundance of possessions" (Luke 12:15). He continued by explaining that it's foolish to store up earthly treasures instead of being rich toward God (12:16–21).

Seeking wealth typically leads us away from God, not toward Him, because, "No one can serve two masters. Either you will hate the one and love the other, or you will be devoted to the one and despise the other. You cannot serve both God and money" (Matt. 6:24).

Other passages also deny that godliness leads to wealth. James 2:1–9 points out that some poor people have more faith than some rich people. Hebrews 13:5 explains that those who know the Lord will keep their lives free from the love of money, being content with what they have. "The love of money is a root of all kinds of evil," and it causes some people to give up their faith. There are many reasons we should flee from worldly values and "pursue righteousness, godliness, faith, love, endurance and gentleness" (1 Tim. 6:10–11).

It is not sinful for Christians to gain wealth if they do so legitimately according to God's purposes, which means they will use it generously and appropriately. But wealth is not a biblical promise. If we find ourselves thinking we deserve certain things in life, we must remember Paul's secret in Philippians 4:12–13, a passage prosperity preachers ignore: "I have learned the secret of being content in any and every situation, whether well fed or hungry, whether living in plenty or in want. I can do all this through him who gives me strength."

If the great apostle Paul went through periods when he had very little, we can be confident that wealth is not a promise for those who have faith.

Christ's Victory Over Death

Let's affirm that Jesus can, and does, heal people. The half-truth we will address is the claim that all Christians are promised healing for any and every health problem they face on earth. My first statement might surprise you: without a doubt, Scripture confirms that Christ's death and resurrection defeated sin, Satan, sickness, and death. Numerous passages tell us it's a done deal.

Jesus "disarmed the powers and authorities" and "made a public spectacle of them, triumphing over them by the cross" (Col. 2:15). He broke "the power of the devil, who had the power of death" (Heb. 2:14, NLT).

Jesus "has destroyed death and has brought life and immortality to light through the gospel" (2 Tim. 1:10). In Isaiah 53:5, we read the prophecy of Christ's suffering, and we're assured, "by his wounds we are healed."

Do these passages assure us that earthly healing is an unqualified promise? No. These passages are only part of the story. We must study all that Scripture teaches about a subject to accurately understand it.

In John 16:33 Jesus explained His coming redemption to His disciples, saying, "I have told you these things, so that in me you may have peace. In this world you will have trouble. But take heart! I have overcome the world." Christ overcame the world on the cross, but He wanted His disciples to know that they would still suffer during their earthly lives.

This truth is further clarified in Romans 8:19–23:

> For the creation waits in eager expectation for the children of God to be revealed. For the creation was subjected to frustration, not by its own choice, but by the will of the one who subjected it, in hope that the creation itself will be liberated from its bondage to decay and brought into the freedom and glory of the children of God. We know that the whole creation has been groaning as in the pains of childbirth right up to the present time. Not only so, but we ourselves, who have the firstfruits of the Spirit, groan inwardly as we wait eagerly for our adoption to sonship, the redemption of our bodies.

We find further confirmation of this in Second Corinthians 4:16–18, which says:

> Therefore we do not lose heart. Though outwardly we are wasting away, yet inwardly we are being renewed day by day. For our light and momentary troubles are achieving for us an eternal glory that far outweighs them all. So we fix our eyes not on what is seen, but on what is unseen, since what is seen is temporary, but what is unseen is eternal.

Again, in Hebrews 2:6–8, we're told that while we're on earth, we won't experience the complete fulfillment of Christ's victory:

> "What is mankind that you are mindful of them,
>   a son of man that you care for him?
> You made them a little lower than the angels;
>   you crowned them with glory and honor
>   and put everything under their feet."
>
> In putting everything under them, God left nothing that is not subject to them. Yet at present we do not see everything subject to them.

And Hebrews 9:28 contains this short explanation: "Christ was sacrificed once to take away the sins of many; and he will appear a second time, not to bear sin, but to bring salvation to those who are waiting for him."

> ***Christ fully accomplished our salvation, and one day we shall fully experience His victory in every area. But during our earthly lives, we continue to deal with our fallen world.***

These verses help us understand that Christ fully accomplished our salvation, and one day we shall fully experience His victory in every area. But during our earthly lives, we continue to deal with our fallen world.

Our earthly environment and our physical bodies are still subject to sin, decay, illness, and physical death. Satan is fully defeated for eternity, but he's still alive and well here on earth. That's why we must have "confidence in what we hope for and assurance about what we do not see" (Heb. 11:1).

Does Faith Heal Us?

Those who claim that all Christians can be healed typically blame illness on a lack of faith, and a half-truth is involved in this claim. Jesus rebuked the disciples for their lack of faith in casting out a demon in Matthew 17:16–21 and commended the Centurion for his faith in believing Jesus could heal his servant (8:5–13). Because the people in His hometown had little faith in Him, Christ didn't do many miracles there (13:53–58). And several times in the Gospels, Jesus credited a person's healing to their faith (e.g., Mark 10:46–52 and Matt. 9:20–22).

If we saw this truth consistently in Scripture, we could believe that those with faith will be healed, and those who lack faith will not be healed. But that's not the full message of Scripture. For example, in Luke 17:11–19 Jesus healed ten lepers but only one thanked Him for the healing, and Jesus only commended that one man for his faith, not the other nine.

Another example is the man who thought his healing was tied to the stirring of the water at the pool of Bethesda (John 5:1–15). We see no evidence in this passage that he had faith before or after his healing. Again, in John 9, a man born blind didn't ask Jesus to heal him nor did he know who Jesus was until after he'd been healed. At that point he came to faith, not before.

The purpose of signs and wonders during Christ's life on earth was to prove He was the Messiah, not simply to feed and heal the crowds (Matt. 8:14–17; Acts 2:22). Some people ignored the true meaning of the signs and simply followed Him for the benefits. That's why in John 6, Christ rebuked the crowd, which He'd miraculously fed, with the words, "I tell you the truth, you want to be with me because I fed you, not because you understood the miraculous signs" (6:26, NLT).

Sin Causes Sickness

James 5:14–18 addresses sickness caused by sin:

> Is anyone among you sick? Let them call the elders of the church to pray over them and anoint them with oil in the name of the Lord. And the prayer offered in faith will make the sick person well; the Lord will raise them up. If they have sinned, they will be forgiven. Therefore confess your sins to each other and pray for each other so that you may be healed. The prayer of a righteous person is powerful and effective.
>
> Elijah was a human being, even as we are. He prayed earnestly that it would not rain, and it did not rain on the land for three and a half years. Again he prayed, and the heavens gave rain, and the earth produced its crops.

If this were the only passage on healing, we could confidently proclaim that all sickness is due to unrepentant sin. We could say repentance followed by faithful, earnest prayer will result in healing. But, as we've learned when studying half-truth teachings, single verses and passages must be combined with all that Scripture teaches. Just as Matthew 7:7 doesn't mean we will receive everything we ask for in prayer, James 5:14–18 is not an unqualified promise for healing. It applies in some situations, but not all situations.

Timothy's Health Problems

Perhaps more than any other passage, First Timothy 5:23 refutes those who claim healing is an unqualified promise for the faithful. In Philippians 2:19–22 and Second Timothy 1:5 Paul praised Timothy, placing great confidence in Timothy's faith and qualifications as a spiritual leader. But in First Timothy 5:23 Paul said to Timothy, "Stop drinking only water, and use a little wine because of your stomach and your frequent illnesses."

If sickness only affects Christians who lack faith or harbor unrepentant sin, why didn't Paul urge Timothy to believe God for his healing or repent of his sins? Paul was an apostle and a divinely inspired teacher, well known for fearlessly rebuking error. But he did not correct or rebuke Timothy. He simply suggested something to help him deal with his frequent illnesses.

Scripture offers other examples as well. In Galatians 4:13–15, Paul spoke of being sick when he preached to the Galatians. In Philippians 2:25–30, Paul talked about Epaphroditus, a faithful servant of God, being so sick that he almost died, and Paul never rebuked him for a lack of faith or a problem with sin. He simply explained that Epaphroditus was healed by God's mercy. Again, in Second Timothy 4:20 Paul said he left a faithful Christian worker and companion sick in Miletus.

In none of these passages did Paul associate sickness to a lack of faith or unrepentant sin. It is no accident that these passages were included by God's Spirit in Scripture. They prove that God does not promise healing in every situation.

Inconsistency

One final consideration is the inconsistency in the claim that all Christians can be healed. Scripture explains that Christ's sacrifice defeated sickness, death, and Satan. If someone teaches that Christ's death frees us from earthly sickness, why do they believe that Christians still experience physical death and still have to contend with Satan here on earth (Eph. 6:10–12)? Pulling sickness out of the list of Christ's accomplishments on the cross is neither honest nor logical.

Eternal Health and Wealth

Scripture tells us that sometimes sickness is related to unrepentant sin or unbelief, but it's often simply a part of our lives in a fallen world. Sometimes God blesses us with earthly wealth, and sometimes He withholds it according to His plans for us. Our wise or unwise decisions can also influence our health and wealth.

Now that I've been a believer for more than fifty years, I can say without hesitation that I've grown more through hard situations than I have when things are going smoothly. Dealing with difficulties strengthens our faith and deepens our trust in God.

Even when we don't fully understand His purposes in our lives, we can trust Him. When we face sickness, untimely death of loved ones, and other hardships and challenges, we can be confident that our earthly lives are a tiny part of our existence, and when they are over, we'll enjoy an eternity of peace and love beyond our imaginations (Heb. 11:13–16). Someday Christ will "wipe every tear from [our] eyes, and there will be no more death or sorrow or crying or pain" (Rev. 21:4, NLT). All those things will be gone forever.

God can and does heal people, but He does so according to His will, not according to ours. Because God is infinite and we're finite, we're not capable of fully understanding everything about healing (1 Cor. 13:12), so we need to quit creating formulas and claiming promises that aren't biblical.

Digging Deeper: Questions for Group or Personal Study

1. How do these passages help you better understand the Christian attitude toward wealth: Proverbs 30:8–9; Second Corinthians 9:9–12; Hebrews 13:16?
2. In Second Corinthians 12:5–10, Paul explains his "thorn" in the flesh. Scholars suggest this could have been a physical ailment, a spiritual attack, or a personal weakness. How does Paul's explanation shed some light on the subject of unsolved problems in life?
3. How does Job 1 offer an alternative purpose in hardships such as physical illness? Note God's view of Job (1:8).
4. Some health problems can be the result of sinful behaviors like gluttony, drugs, or alcohol. But many health problems have no direct relationship to personal sin. When someone blames a person's health on sin without legitimate reasons, they echo the accusations of Job's friends. See what God said about this in Job 42:7–8.
5. Has your faith in God been strengthened through personal health problems? Or has it been strengthened by observing how other Christians deal with health problems? Are you able to share with others how you grew through these situations?
6. Healing is one of the spiritual gifts listed in First Corinthians 12:7–11. What insights do this passage and Hebrews 2:1–4 offer in this regard?
7. What Scriptures in this chapter would be most helpful to remember when explaining the biblical view of healing?

Section 3

Half-Truths about Sexual Behavior

When cultures move away from God, sexual immorality is usually at the forefront. A great deal of half-truth propaganda is required to justify these unnatural and unhealthy sexual relationships.

12

Half-Truth: "Tolerance Means Approval"

OUR CULTURE HAS gradually accepted and promoted increasingly immoral views about sexual intimacy, and those views have led to a new half-truth definition of tolerance. This new definition is used as a self-righteous shaming tool to promote uniformity of thought.

No One Is Neutral

Recently, I heard someone who was promoting abortion and LGBTQ+ lifestyles say, "The tolerant must not tolerate the intolerant." If this meant that tolerant people must not tolerate disagreements that lead to violence or mistreatment, I would agree wholeheartedly. But the context clearly revealed that the person was saying, "We must not tolerate those who don't approve of *my* values."

This popular view of tolerance not only changes the true meaning of the word, it contradicts it. And it reinforces culture's half-truth definitions of "love" and "hate."

Intolerant tolerance has been around a long time. This basic tactic of propaganda is behind most totalitarian takeovers of nations, because controlling people's view of right and wrong is the first step in completely controlling their lives.

The problem with expecting uniformity in a culture is the fact that no one is neutral. We may have no opinion about a sports team or a flavor of ice cream, but adults are never neutral about lifestyles and religions. We all have preferences, beliefs, and convictions, some of which we hold strongly. That's why genuine tolerance is necessary.

But genuine tolerance doesn't mean accepting all beliefs. It means treating all people humanely even if we disagree. Scripture offers the perfect definition: "In everything, do to others what you would have them do to you, for this sums up the Law and the Prophets" (Matt. 7:12).

Genuine tolerance is about handling our differences humanely and graciously. It's not about approval, agreement, or silence.

This means we share our beliefs appropriately, without mockery, sarcasm, or name-calling. It means we shouldn't force others to agree with us, nor should they force us to agree with them. It's about handling our differences humanely and graciously. It's not about approval, agreement, or silence.

Christians should treat people without harshness or mistreatment, even if we disagree with their lifestyles, religious beliefs, and politics. And the same is true for those who disagree with us.

This doesn't mean we stop hating what is evil, as we're called to do in Romans 12:9. We continue to hate false teachings, which violate God's loving commands, misrepresent His character, and lead people to destruction.

We don't adjust our beliefs to please others, nor do we mistreat those who disagree with us. We can hate beliefs without hating the people who hold them.

Those who promote intolerant tolerance claim that our refusal to accept LGBTQ+ lifestyles makes people who follow those lifestyles feel rejected and causes them emotional problems. If this were true, Christians could also claim we're harmed by rejection of our beliefs, especially since our world culture is far more negative about Christian views than about LGBTQ+ views.

There has never been a culture, nation, or even a neighborhood where everyone agrees with everyone about everything.

Tolerance isn't about approval. For example, business owners should be able to set rules for work areas and other venues where their employees represent the company. A Jewish business owner shouldn't be forced to allow employees to display swastika symbols while at work. And Christian business owners shouldn't be forced to allow employees to promote or display things which dishonor Christian beliefs (e.g., pornography, gay pride flags, or pagan symbols). Employees may not agree with the owner's beliefs, but they shouldn't be allowed to mock those beliefs while on the job.

We've seen lawsuits brought against Christian business owners who refused to violate their consciences by catering homosexual weddings, and we need to recognize the hypocrisy in such suits. Imagine a Christian group demanding that a gay business owner cater their seminar teaching that homosexuality is an ungodly perversion. I'm sure the gay business would not cater the seminar, and culture would side with the gay business.

We live in a world blinded by Satan's lies, so we shouldn't be surprised that Muslims, Hindus, atheists, and LGBTQ+ advocates are not the main target of intolerant tolerance. Satan's greatest mission is to damage Christianity, and he'd like to "bully" us into silence. That is why we must hold firmly to the conviction Paul expressed in Romans 1:16: "I am not ashamed of the gospel, because it is the power of God that brings salvation to everyone who believes."

Scriptures to Help Us Remain Genuinely Tolerant

With this constant opposition, Christians must refuse to deny God's Word, even if it brings us insult or rejection. God tells us to be on our guard, stand firm, and be courageous and strong (1 Cor. 16:13). We need not depend on our own power. We can depend on God's power (Eph. 6:10).

God also comforts us with the truth that when we're persecuted and insulted for the sake of righteousness, we are blessed (Matt. 5:10–12). So let's "run with perseverance the race marked out for us, fixing our eyes on Jesus, the pioneer and perfecter of faith" (Heb. 12:1–2). Jesus said, "They hated me without reason," and He said we should expect the same (John 15:18–25). The purpose of propaganda in Christ's day and in ours is to demonize certain views and glorify others.

Sadly, the prevalent propaganda in today's culture is successfully changing public opinion and leading some professing Christians to walk away from their faith (Matt. 24:12–13). But other Christians are not giving in to these pressures. We're standing firm and remembering Hebrews 13:6: "The Lord is my helper; I will not be afraid. / What can mere mortals do to me?"

As our culture declines and our views become less popular, we must "be as shrewd as snakes and as innocent as doves" (Matt. 10:16). That means we seek God's wisdom when facing half-truth propaganda in the church and when sharing Christ with the unsaved. We must never allow the world's intolerance to silence us, but we must contend for our faith wisely and strategically.

Identifying With Jeremiah

If you are faithfully sharing God's truth in the midst of our anti-Christian culture, you will identify with Jeremiah's lament: "The word of the LORD has brought me / insult and reproach all day long. / But if I say, 'I will not mention his word / or speak anymore in his name,' / his word is in my heart like a fire . . . I am weary of holding it in; / indeed, I cannot" (Jer. 20:8–9).

As we face increasing bullying and censorship, each of us must make some important choices. We can keep silent and make Jesus ashamed of us (Mark 8:38). Or we can depend on our human reasoning and worldly philosophies and foolishly join those who redefine God's truth (1 Cor. 3:19).

> ***We can't force God on the world, but we must be careful not to let the world force their foolishness on us.***

Or we can love Jesus enough to stand for His truth, no matter the cost. Jesus clearly defined those who love Him in John 14:23: "Anyone who loves me will obey my teaching. My Father will love them, and we will come to them and make our home with them."

God's Word is pure wisdom. Every principle and command is loving, pure, and right. We can't force God on the world, but we must be careful not to let the world force their foolishness on us.

Digging Deeper: Questions for Group or Personal Study

1. Suppose you are teaching a Bible study that addresses sex from a biblical perspective with warnings against premarital sex, pornography, adultery, and homosexuality. You want to advertise your class on social media, but you know some platforms "hide" posts that share biblical views of sex and gender. How could you be both honest and shrewd (Matt. 10:16)?

2. What are some practical ways you can apply First Corinthians 16:13 and First Peter 1:13 to your life?

3. Consider memorizing one or all of these verses to help you face the anti-Christian climate in our world: Matthew 5:10; 10:22; Ephesians 6:10.

4. I've consistently shown love for some people for years only to have them proudly and bitterly cut me off when I've disagreed with their views on abortion or LGBTQ+ lifestyles. Others tell me they have also experienced this behavior. How does James 4:4–6 give us insights into these situations?

5. How do these passages help us deal with those who bully and mistreat us for our faith: First Peter 3:9; Romans 12:21; Matthew 5:44; Luke 6:28?

13

The Beginning

WHEN ROMANS 1:18–32 describes the depravity of mankind, sexual sins play a prominent role. We are rightly concerned with the personal and cultural damage that comes from approving LGBTQ+ lifestyles, but our moral decline did not begin there. The approval of premarital sex laid the groundwork for increasingly harmful sexual sins. So, let's look at the beginning of our decline into sexual perversion.

Half-Truth: "Premarital Sex Is Normal and Natural"

God created us as sexual beings, but He designed sexual intimacy for one man and one woman married to each other (Gen. 2:21–25; Matt. 19:5). Because He's our designer, He knows what brings us the greatest fulfillment, safety, and love.

As we discussed in Chapter 10, sexual sins are more damaging than other sins. Sadly, our world now fully approves premarital sex to the point that living together before marriage is the norm, not the exception. And studies show that many professing Christians have followed culture instead of Scripture.[1]

> Run from sexual sin! No other sin so clearly affects the body as this one does. For sexual immorality is a sin against your

1 Juliana Menasce Horowitz, Nikki Graf, and Gretchen Livingston, "Why people get married or move in with a partner," Pew Research Center (https://www.pewresearch.org/social-trends/2019/11/06/why-people-get-married-or-move-in-with-a-partner/), accessed June 16, 2025.

> own body. Don't you realize that your body is the temple of the Holy Spirit, who lives in you and was given to you by God? You do not belong to yourself, for God bought you with a high price. So you must honor God with your body. (1 Cor. 6:18–20, NLT)

I remember the first time I realized how much immoral attitudes had infiltrated the church. I was in my forties and teaching a Bible study to a group of young moms in their twenties and thirties. When I explained what the Bible teaches about premarital sex, one young mom took me aside after class and told me I was old-fashioned to think that genuine believers wouldn't live together before marriage.

A few years later, I read a news story that further revealed the compromised "Christian" attitude toward premarital sex. The article was about a Christian school that required students to sign a pledge of purity. If students violated the pledge, they could not participate in certain extracurricular privileges.

When one student got pregnant, several parents and students claimed her "mistake" shouldn't affect her privileges at the school. Instead of encouraging her to feel sorrow for her sin (James 4:7–10), they focused on the fact that she didn't get an abortion.

We should never encourage people to call their sins "mistakes," nor should we overlook one sin because they didn't commit another.

Scripture explains that when Christians sin, they'll feel the conviction of the Holy Spirit, which leads them to repentance. We should never encourage people to call their sins "mistakes," nor should we overlook one sin because they didn't commit another.

God's Word clarifies that "no one who continues to sin has either seen [Christ] or known him" (1 John 3:6). Our love for Christ compels us to obey His loving and purposeful commands.

Scripture never expresses a casual attitude toward sexual sin; instead it emphasizes the opposite:

> Neither the sexually immoral nor idolaters nor adulterers nor men who have sex with men nor thieves nor the greedy nor drunkards nor slanderers nor swindlers will inherit the kingdom of God. And that is what some of you were. But you were washed, you were sanctified, you were justified in the name of the Lord Jesus Christ and by the Spirit of our God. (1 Cor. 6:9–11)

Half-Truth: "Sometimes the Temptation is Too Strong"

People who sin sexually often say they were caught off guard or overwhelmed in a moment of passion. But that's never the case. Scripture tells us every sin has two steps: first, thoughts, and then, actions.

Whenever we entertain lustful thoughts instead of fighting them, we sin (Matt. 5:28). This is why pornography is sinful whether it leads to immoral acts or not. But sexual sins always begin in the mind, and entertaining those lustful thoughts is the first step in carrying them out. The thoughts may come months or only a few minutes before the sinful act, but they are always the first step.

> For out of the heart come evil thoughts—murder, adultery, sexual immorality, theft, false testimony, slander. (15:19)
>
> Then, after desire has conceived, it gives birth to sin. (James 1:15)

Step one is entertaining immoral thoughts, and step two is refusing God's "exit plan." You see, God promises to give us a way out of any temptation, but we must choose to take it (1 Cor. 10:13). Sexual sin isn't an overpowering passion, an accident, or a mistake. It's a premeditated, sinful choice—a choice we can reject with the Lord's help.

These truths also apply to any extramarital sex. Adultery is condemned in both the Old and New Testaments because "Marriage should be honored by all, and the marriage bed kept pure, for God will judge the adulterer and all the sexually immoral"

(Heb. 13:4). No matter what the world tells us, the most fulfilling, purposeful, loving, safe relationships are those that follow God's biblical commands for sexual intimacy.

Half-Truth: "It's My Body"

Before going further, I want to speak to those who have had an abortion: Please seek godly counsel from a mature Christian who is trained in postabortion syndrome. I know women who had abortions, confessed their sin, and received God's forgiveness, but they still needed to process what had happened before they could be truly free of the weight of this sin.

One of the most tragic consequences of the cultural acceptance of premarital sex is that babies are conceived in casual, noncommitted relationships. And many of those babies are aborted. Pro-abortion groups typically highlight the 1.5 percent of abortions done as a result of rape or incest. And they highlight the small percentage done for underage teens. But statistics show that most abortions are done on adult women aged 20 or older simply because they choose to have irresponsible, unprotected sex.

Perhaps the greatest lie in the pro-abortion movement is their claim to be "pro-choice." Pro-life crisis pregnancy centers typically offer a number of choices, such as free medical services, financial help, and counseling. And one of their goals is to help the woman make an educated choice based on a full understanding of the child forming in her womb and what abortion involves.

In contrast, the pro-abortion movement consistently opposes any legislation that lets a woman see an ultrasound of her unborn baby. Pro-abortionists don't want women making educated choices because part of that education is recognizing that they have their son or daughter in the womb.

The main area in which the pro-abortion movement is "pro-choice" is allowing a woman to choose when to kill her child. Pro-abortionists oppose all time restrictions. The woman can do it before anyone knows she's pregnant, or she can wait until her child is fully formed and able to live outside the womb. There is no reason for taking this long to have an abortion, but it definitely increases the brutality of the abortion method causing the fully formed child to feel intense pain. And since the abortion industry won't admit they are killing a *child,* they won't do anything to alleviate the pain of the child's torturous death.

Many women who have abortions live with long-term emotional problems. A woman instinctively knows she has killed her own child, and most women have lingering doubts and guilt. Instead of warning women about this, pro-abortion groups often deny the problem exists. So pro-life groups pick up the pieces, counseling and comforting those with postabortion syndrome.

Half-Truth: "Scripture Says Nothing About Abortion"

The word "abortion" is not used in Scripture, but this is an irrelevant excuse since many methods of murder are not specifically mentioned in the Bible. But God's Word is 100 percent clear about the taking of innocent life.

God gives each of us life, according to His timing and purposes (Acts 17:26–28). Multiple passages explain that God creates a person at the moment of conception. Perhaps the most popular is Psalm 139:13–16:

> For you created my inmost being;
> you knit me together in my mother's womb.
> I praise you because I am fearfully and wonderfully made;
> your works are wonderful,
> I know that full well.
> My frame was not hidden from you
> when I was made in the secret place,
> when I was woven together in the depths of the earth.
> Your eyes saw my unformed body;
> all the days ordained for me were written in your book
> before one of them came to be.

Despite this clear explanation of God's hand in our creation, which is similarly expressed in Job 31:15, Isaiah 44:2, 49:5, and Luke 1:41–44, some people claim that the unborn child isn't a child until the second trimester. But the Christian cannot use this excuse.

Psalm 139 does not say, "For you created my inmost being *after the first trimester*; *after three-and-a-half months of pregnancy*, you knit me together in my mother's womb . . . all the days ordained for me were written in your book—*but not until I'd been in my mother's womb for ninety-six days*."

Jeremiah 1:5 puts this first trimester excuse to rest, explaining, "Before I formed you in the womb I knew you, / before you were born I set you apart; / I appointed you as a prophet to the nations." God specifically decides who will be conceived in each mother's womb. He knows who will be aborted, but that is never His will.

Some people who fight passionately against the mistreatment of animals approve of brutal late-term abortions. This is hypocrisy at the highest level.

The Ten Commandments (Exod. 20:13) and many other Scripture passages condemn the murder of innocent people. And abortion is clearly the murder of an innocent child.

It's ironic that many people who approve abortion also oppose the death penalty, even for those who commit heinous crimes. And some people who fight passionately against the mistreatment of animals approve of brutal late-term abortions. This is hypocrisy at the highest level.

Abortion is simply an atheistic, humanistic method of child sacrifice, something condemned in Scripture (e.g., Lev. 18:21 and 20:2–5). Instead of offering children to idols to gain something from a pagan god, our culture sacrifices children to the gods of convenience, finances, or reputation. Abortion defiles any nation that approves it.

> They sacrificed their sons
> and their daughters to false gods.
> They shed innocent blood,
> the blood of their sons and daughters,
> whom they sacrificed to the idols of Canaan,
> and the land was desecrated by their blood.
> (Ps. 106:37–38)

Exodus 21:22 Propaganda

If someone comes to you with a teaching based on a single Old Testament passage, beware! One such example is the false claim that Exodus 21:22 proves an unborn child is not fully human:

> If people are fighting and hit a pregnant woman and she gives birth prematurely but there is no serious injury, the offender must be fined whatever the woman's husband demands and the court allows.

During this time in Israel's history, *lex talionis* (reciprocal justice) was the law of the land, requiring that the punishment resemble the offense—so in cases of murder, it was a life for a life (Lev. 24:19–21). A few translations, however, use the word "miscarriage" instead of premature birth in Exodus 21:22. Pro-abortion advocates have latched onto those few translations using miscarriage, insisting that since the murderer was fined and not killed, it proves that God does not view an unborn baby the same as a person already born.

It's a common tactic of false teachers to take one passage out of context and claim it presents a truth that contradicts scores of other Bible verses. Besides the passages listed in the section above that share God's view of unborn life, an Old Testament law also refutes this pro-abortion claim about the woman miscarrying.

If the woman had actually miscarried, it would have been an unintentional murder of the baby, and the murderer could flee to a city of refuge. This law for unintentional murders is found in the same chapter: Exodus 21:12–14.

Using Exodus 21:22 to form a false doctrine is one of many examples of the extent to which people will go to justify a sin. And in this case, they absurdly compare an accidental miscarriage to the premeditated murder of an innocent child in an abortion clinic.

Just as many American slave owners twisted a few out-of-context Scriptures in the 1800s to claim that slaves were less than human and unworthy of freedom, pro-abortion groups claim unborn children are less than human and unworthy of life.

Both slavery and abortion are evil practices that deny the Golden Rule: "In everything, do to others what you would have them do to you" (Matt. 7:12). I highly doubt that slave owners would have offered to be slaves to help a friend or neighbor make a better living. And I doubt that women seeking abortions would offer their lives to make things easier for another person.

I'm grateful for the faithful Christians who fought against slavery, and I'm also grateful for the faithful Christians who fight against abortion.

Half-Truth: "Without Legal Abortion, Many Women Will Die"

In extremely rare cases, a woman's life might be threatened if she carries her baby full term. But abortion laws in the U.S. do not prevent the saving of a pregnant woman's life. In fact, long before abortion was legal, the Comstock Law, passed in 1873, made therapeutic abortions legal if pregnancy and childbirth threatened the woman's life.

Despite this clear truth, pro-abortion groups continue to use "life-of-the-mother" arguments as a scare tactic, even claiming that prohibiting abortion would mean women who miscarry couldn't get adequate medical help.

Two other facts are important in addressing this lie. With modern medical procedures, many doctors believe it's almost never necessary to choose between mother and child. And when they do, it's not called an abortion. An abortion has only one aim: to kill the unborn child. Procedures to save the mother's life seek to save both mother and child.

Half-Truth: "Abortion Is Necessary for Rape and Incest Victims"

These are the most difficult cases, and though they only comprise 1.5 percent of all abortions, they deserve our concern. We should want such cases to be handled carefully, causing the least problems for the victims. But allowing the unborn child to be killed is still playing God and presumes God cannot redeem a horrible situation. In addition, abortion can deepen a woman's trauma instead of alleviating it, causing her to suffer from post-abortion guilt. And abortion in the case of incest sometimes allows the abuser to continue abusing, where a pregnancy would reveal his evil behavior to the authorities.

Those who genuinely believe abortion should be allowed only for rape and incest should still be opposed to abortion for other reasons. If people approve laws allowing abortion for any reason, they are saying that for every three women who are raped or are victims of incest, *200* innocent babies should give their lives—three babies carried by raped women (1.5 percent) and 197 babies killed for other reasons (98.5 percent).

The Full Truth

Let me end this difficult chapter with these truths: God has given us a wonderful, fulfilling way to express our love and intimacy in marriage. When we deny that design through premarital or extramarital sex, we damage the well-being of our bodies, souls, and spirits. And we create problems that cause us to commit more serious sins, such as murder of the unborn.

Digging Deeper: Questions for Group or Personal Study

1. What damage is done when we have sex before marriage? If you are guilty of this sin, have you taken it to the Lord and fully repented? If so, how has God helped you find peace in that area?
2. Have you ever considered how the acceptance of a smaller sin leads to acceptance of a greater sin? Have you seen this happen in your life or the life of loved ones?
3. If someone told you that they want abortion legalized because someone they knew was raped and it was important that she get an abortion, how would you respond?
4. Why do you think abortion has become such a pivotal issue in our world? Why do you think it was so rapidly approved and legalized after so many centuries of disapproval?
5. What do Leviticus 18:21, Deuteronomy 12:31, and Ezekiel 16:20–21 reveal about the practice of abortion?

14

LGBTQ+ Lifestyles and Lies

SATAN'S PURPOSE IS to steal, kill, and destroy, and Scripture warns us that he blinds the minds of unbelievers (John 10:10; 2 Cor. 4:4). Of course, Christ can still reach the blinded mind of unbelievers if they open their hearts to His message, but Satan is always seeking to take mankind deeper into darkness, helping people approve and embrace unnatural—and even absurd—forms of sin.

After successfully blinding culture to the soul damage of premarital sex and abortion, Satan went on to encourage types of perversion that cause God to "give people over" to their sins. That is the only reason why the LGBTQ+ movement came about.

Physically blind people cannot see the obstacles and dangers in their path, and that's true for the spiritually blind as well. Whatever pleasure people gain from immorality is nothing compared to the destruction it brings their hearts and souls. And Satan's greatest pleasure is seeing men and women choose hell instead of God's forgiveness and salvation.

When we understand these truths, we realize that nothing is loving about remaining silent while people choose LGBTQ+ lifestyles. We can tell them how to find forgiveness, be set free from their destructive choices, and receive eternal life. If we remain silent, they'll blindly walk to their spiritual death.

We know many of them will reject what we share about Christ, but it's loving to at least give them a chance. Contrary to cultural rhetoric, it's hateful *not* to share God's truth about sexually perverse lifestyles. If we had the cure for a disease, no one would call us loving if we kept that cure to ourselves. But that's exactly what the world expects us to do in regard to the saving power of the gospel.

What Scripture Teaches

Before looking at some of the half-truths and outright lies used to defend and promote LGBTQ+ lifestyles, let's look at what Scripture clearly teaches.

The Old Testament Only Approves Heterosexual Married Partners

Throughout the Old Testament, any type of sex outside of heterosexual marriage was condemned with strong warnings that it defiles whole nations (e.g., Lev. 18:22–24). Even though Christ fulfilled the dietary, sacrificial, cleansing, and ceremonial laws when He died for our sins, the Old Testament laws still hold important principles regarding moral behavior.

For example, Leviticus 20:13 says, "If a man has sexual relations with a man as one does with a woman, both of them have done what is detestable. They are to be put to death; their blood will be on their own heads." We are no longer commanded to kill homosexuals—that was a specific civil law for a specific time in Israel's history. But the principle behind the law is permanent—homosexuality is sinful, bringing damage to individuals who practice it and to communities that approve it.

New Testament Commands Against Homosexuality

If someone doubts the permanence or validity of Old Testament laws against homosexuality, that's not a problem. God's views of perversion are also very clear in the New Testament.

Romans 1:16–32 talks about the decline of a culture, and homosexuality is a key element in that decline.

> ***Throughout history, Christians have been mocked and shamed for holding biblical views about sexual behavior.***

Paul begins this section of Romans 1 by proclaiming, "I am not ashamed of the gospel, because it is the power of God that brings salvation to everyone who believes" (Rom. 1:16). It's fitting to start with this statement since throughout history, Christians have been mocked and shamed for holding biblical views about sexual behavior. So Paul starts with this affirmation of the gospel and proceeds to give a strong message about God's wrath and the sins that destroy cultures.

Romans 1:26–27 (NLT) specifically talks about homosexual behavior:

> God abandoned them to their shameful desires. Even the women turned against the natural way to have sex and instead indulged in sex with each other. And the men, instead of having normal sexual relations with women, burned with lust for each other. Men did shameful things with other men, and as a result of this sin, they suffered within themselves the penalty they deserved.

Romans 1:32 says, "Although they know God's righteous decree that those who do such things deserve death, they not only continue to do these very things but also approve of those who practice them." Gay pride goes even further than approval. It celebrates these harmful sins that corrupt people and nations.

Romans 1 also removes any excuses we may have for why people choose sinful behavior. Romans 1:18–20 tells us that people experience God's wrath because they

> . . . suppress the truth by their wickedness, since what may be known about God is plain to them, because God has made it

> plain to them. For since the creation of the world God's invisible qualities—his eternal power and divine nature—have been clearly seen, being understood from what has been made, so that people are without excuse.

The human body clearly reveals God's design for sexual intimacy between one man and one woman.

Because Romans 1 is so clear and specific, it's hard to refute. That's why some compromised Christians have resorted to calling Romans 1 and similar passages "clobber passages," as if they shouldn't be used in discussing LGBTQ+ issues because they're too harsh. But if Romans 1 "clobbers" anyone, it's clobbering them with life-saving truth that can rescue their souls and set them free from the bondage of sin and death.

If we care about people's souls, we won't sugarcoat the truth and "comfort" them with Satan's hateful lies. We'll warn them of God's judgment and help them seek forgiveness and new life in Christ. If Romans 1 is not convincing enough, Scripture also tells us that practicing homosexuals cannot be saved if they don't repent:

> Don't you realize that those who do wrong will not inherit the Kingdom of God? Don't fool yourselves. Those who indulge in sexual sin, or who worship idols, or commit adultery, or are male prostitutes, or practice homosexuality, or are thieves, or greedy people, or drunkards, or are abusive, or cheat people—none of these will inherit the Kingdom of God. Some of you were once like that. But you were cleansed; you were made holy; you were made right with God by calling on the name of the Lord Jesus Christ and by the Spirit of our God. (1 Cor. 6:9–11, NLT)

Please note that this very strong condemnation ends with the beautiful grace of the gospel: No matter how evil our lifestyles, if we repent and turn to the Lord, we can be saved.

But What About Transgenderism?

Years ago, no one would have imagined that Genesis 1:27 and Mark 10:6 would become controversial Bible passages: "God created mankind in his own image, / in the image of God he created them; / male and female he created them." Sadly, these biblical truths are now under attack.

While transgenderism usually includes homosexual behavior, it's important to note that seeking to live as another gender or medically seeking to change our gender is sinful, whether it involves sexual intimacy or not. Furthermore, it's a result of serious propaganda—and especially dangerous when introduced to underage children.

> ***Our gender is no accident. God created us in the womb, designing us to be male or female from the beginning. We damage our souls when we defy God's gender choice.***

Sinful transvestic behavior (gaining sexual pleasure from cross-dressing) has been around for a long time, but transgenderism is a new trend and a deadly one. It might best be described as a "fad" among people who will live to regret unalterable decisions they've made with their physical bodies.

Our gender is no accident. God created us in the womb, designing us to be male or female from the beginning (Ps. 139:13–16). We damage our souls when we defy God's gender choice: "What sorrow awaits those who argue with their Creator. / Does a clay pot argue with its maker? / Does the clay dispute with the one who shapes it, saying, / 'Stop, you're doing it wrong!'" (Isa. 45:9, NLT).

We have different personalities, interests, skills, and mannerisms. Not every man needs to be ruggedly masculine, nor every woman lacy feminine. But God assigns gender, and He knows us better than we know ourselves (Ps. 139). We will study First Corinthians 6:9–10 more thoroughly in the next chapter.

Sharing Truth In Love

We've already talked about the fact that it's loving to warn people of things that damage their hearts and souls, so sharing what the Bible teaches is a loving thing to do. But it's also important to share these truths graciously.

We need to let God's Spirit guide our speech and show us the best time and place to speak up. If the person is a family member, we need to let them know that we still love them, but we can't approve of their choices. We can and should remain friends with our loved ones who are involved in ungodly lifestyles, as long as we don't do anything that validates or affirms their sexual behavior.

For example, Christians should not attend LGBTQ+ weddings because these ceremonies celebrate lifestyles that defy God's loving commands. Those who attend are honoring a choice that damages their loved one's heart and soul. Such ceremonies would qualify as the "fruitless deeds of darkness," which Christians must avoid (Eph. 5:1–14).

My husband and I have moved frequently for ministry purposes, and we often look for a new church by listening to online sermons before visiting. It's especially helpful to find a sermon on Romans 1 or other passages that address homosexuality. We want a pastor who offers a balance of truth and love in addressing this culturally approved sin.

Sadly, we've heard more sermons that soften the strong, clear teaching of these passages. Such pastors say little about praying for LGBTQ+ people and speaking God's truth about this sin that sends them to hell.

Culture has a powerful influence on Christians, but we must refuse to give in to cultural philosophies that deny God's Word. If God strongly warns us about certain sins in His Word, telling us that they cause Him to "give people over," we should heed His warnings and not ignore or soften them.

Digging Deeper: Questions for Group or Personal Study

1. The practice of homosexuality has affected people and nations throughout history. When approved, it typically has signaled the end of the culture's power and prominence. What truths in Scripture help us understand that approval of a sexual lifestyle can ruin a culture?

2. Why do you think some parents who don't allow their children to choose their bedtime or diet, *do* allow them to choose their gender? Consider these biblical principles: Proverbs 19:18; 22:15; Ephesians 6:4; First Corinthians 13:11; 14:20.

3. In 1973, secular psychology changed its view of homosexuality, removing it from a list of mental illnesses. Why do you think this happened? See Proverbs 1:7, Romans 1:32, and First Corinthians 1:18–21 for insights.

4. If you have a family member who has chosen an LGBTQ+ lifestyle, can you share positive or negative things about how you've handled this situation? Have you found any resources that help you engage your family member in meaningful conversation? Christians should be discussing these things and helping each other to handle them biblically, not culturally.

5. No one is immune from Satan's propaganda unless they are grounded in God's Word. Even many older people, those who were born in a more traditional era, were raised in godly families, and attended church all their lives, now accept immoral elements of culture. How can we protect ourselves from the compromise of cultural pressures? See Romans 12:1–2 and Ephesians 4:17–24.

15

Gay Revisionist Half-Truth Teachings

A GROWING MOVEMENT in the church seeks to justify LGBTQ+ lifestyles by redefining or revising Scripture. Using sophisticated half-truths, those spearheading this movement misrepresent themselves as Bible scholars.[1]

The church must be equipped to refute false beliefs and to stand firm, knowing that God's commands are good, healthy, and loving; they prevent men and women from damaging their souls. Let's look at the specific claims of these people, so we can be prepared to answer them biblically (1 Pet. 3:15–16).

A Truth Twisted: "It's Not Good for Man to Be Alone"

Let's start at the beginning, with the Genesis account of creation. God created male and female, commanding them to be fruitful and increase in number (Gen. 1:27–28). Then, in Genesis 2, God said, "It is not good for the man to be alone. I will make a helper suitable for him" (2:18). So God created woman and said, "That is why a man leaves his father and mother and is united to his wife, and they become one flesh" (2:24).

1 One leader of this movement is Matthew Vines, whose speech "The Gay Debate: The Bible and Homosexuality" went viral on the Internet when he was a 21-year-old college student fourteen years ago (https://matthewvines.com/transcript/), accessed June 16, 2025.

This gives us a clear definition of marriage and intimate relationships: The relationship involves one man and his "suitable helper," one woman. They are designed to physically procreate.

None of these basics can be applied to gay relationships, but revisionists pull out the phrase, "It is not good for the man to be alone" and insist God would want people with homosexual desires to get married. This is clearly an absurd argument that denies God's clear design.

Half-Truth: "The Word 'Homosexual' Isn't in the Bible"

Another gay revisionist argument is claiming the word "homosexual" didn't appear in English Bible translations until the twentieth century. They claim it was added by prejudiced Christians who wanted to discredit a behavior God approved.

This claim is half true. The English word "homosexual" didn't come into normal use until the twentieth century, and it wasn't used in Bible translations until 1946. But when it was used, it accurately translated the original language texts.

Compare these translations of Leviticus 18:22:

> *Wycliffe Bible* (hand-printed about 1382): "Thou shalt not be meddled, [(or) mingled,] with a man, by lechery of a woman, for it is abomination. (Thou shalt not be mixed together with a man, like in fleshly coupling with a woman, for it is an abomination.)"
>
> *Geneva Bible* (1599): "Thou shalt not lie with the male as one lieth with a woman: for it is abomination."
>
> *King James Version* (1611): "Thou shalt not lie with mankind, as with womankind: it is abomination."
>
> *American Standard Version* (1885): "Thou shalt not lie with mankind, as with womankind: it is abomination."
>
> *Revised Standard Version* (1971): "You shall not lie with a male as with a woman; it is an abomination."
>
> *New Living Translation* (2015): "Do not practice homosexuality, having sex with another man as with a woman. It is a detestable sin."

For over six hundred years, the English translations have shared the same message about homosexuality, and this applies to all verses that address homosexuality, in both the Old and New Testaments. Updating language is a legitimate aspect of Bible translation. Even more importantly, all of these translations accurately express the meaning of the original languages of the most reliable Bible manuscripts.

> ***We update translations not to change the truths in God's Word but to make them more understandable to current readers.***

Pull out an old translation of Scripture and you'll find "thees" and "thous," along with words like *adjure*, *anon*, *assay*, *bewray*, *broid*, *haply*, and *wot*. These words were understood when the translations were written, but they aren't recognized by most modern readers. We update translations not to change the truths in God's Word but to make them more understandable to current readers.

The words "homosexual" and "homosexuality" are also used in some New Testament verses, such as in First Timothy 1:10 and First Corinthians 6:9, translating the Greek word *arsenokoites*, which means "a male engaging in same-gender sexual activity."

Half-Truth: "Jesus Never Mentioned Sexual Lifestyles"

It's popular to claim that Bible authors weren't divinely inspired, so only Christ's words can be trusted. Of course, those who hold this belief fail to realize that the words of Christ were recorded by the very Bible authors they don't trust!

Also, Christ's words tell us to expect God's Spirit to teach us further truths—which He did, through the divinely inspired Word of God.

> I have much more to say to you, more than you can now bear. But when he, the Spirit of truth, comes, he will guide you into all the truth. He will not speak on his own; he will speak only what he hears, and he will tell you what is yet to come. (John 16:12–13)

But even a person who only trusts Christ's words will find that Christ clearly affirms God's original design and purpose for marriage and sexual intimacy. When the Pharisees asked him about divorce, Jesus explained,

> "Haven't you read . . . that at the beginning the Creator 'made them male and female,' and said, 'For this reason a man will leave his father and mother and be united to his wife, and the two will become one flesh'? So they are no longer two, but one flesh. Therefore what God has joined together, let no one separate." (Matt. 19:4–6)

Half-Truth: "Only Abuse Is Sinful"

Another gay revisionist claim is that the Bible supports monogamous homosexual relationships and only prohibits abusive homosexual acts. In handling this false teaching, we need to first address some specifics about First Corinthians 6:9–10, the verse they use most often to make this claim. If you read this passage in multiple versions, you will find that some translations list homosexuality directly after adultery. For example, the NIV:

> Or do you not know that wrongdoers will not inherit the kingdom of God? Do not be deceived: Neither the sexually immoral nor idolaters nor adulterers nor men who have sex with men nor thieves nor the greedy nor drunkards nor slanderers nor swindlers will inherit the kingdom of God.

And some translations list "effeminate" or "male prostitute" between adulterers and homosexuals. For example, the NASB 1995:

> Or do you not know that the unrighteous will not inherit the kingdom of God? Do not be deceived; neither fornicators, nor idolaters, nor adulterers, nor effeminate [*malakos*], nor homosexuals

> [*arsenokoitasis*], nor thieves, nor *the* covetous, nor drunkards, nor revilers, nor swindlers, will inherit the kingdom of God.

I'm not sure why some translations combine both words and simply define them as homosexuals ("men who have sex with men"), but the words have separate meanings. *Malakos* translates as "soft, delicate, or effeminate." This word is only found three times in the Bible, and the other two times, Jesus used it to contrast the strength and character of John the Baptist with men living a "soft," luxurious life and wearing expensive clothes (Matt. 11:8; Luke 7:25).

Bible scholars disagree about the exact meaning Paul meant to convey in First Corinthians 6 when he used this word. But we know that *malakos* was used in some Greek texts to mean the passive partner in a homosexual relationship, the partner playing the role of the woman, a homosexual prostitute, or simply a sexual pervert. *Arsenokoitai* is more easily defined, meaning "a male engaging in same-gender sexual activity."

I offer these details because gay revisionists claim this combination denotes sexual exploitation, not normal homosexual relationships. They like to quote the phrase used in the King James Version's translation describing homosexuals as "abusers of themselves with mankind." And some revisionists claim that *malakos* are victims and *arsenokoitai* are victimizers.

Therefore, they insist this passage only condemns homosexual abusers or homosexual prostitutes. Like other revisionist arguments, they want us to believe that for thousands of years, Bible scholars misunderstood or misrepresented these words. But their claim quickly breaks down when the full passage is examined.

The Greek conjunction *oute* is found between each sinful lifestyle mentioned. You don't need to be an idolatrous fornicator or a drunken reviler to be sinful. Each description stands alone. *Malakos* and *arsenokoitai* are condemned separately. And claiming that *malakos* represents victims is absurd because God does not hold victims responsible for acts forced upon them.

This passage clearly defines two types of sinful behavior. The first type can have a variety of meanings ranging from transvestic behavior to transgenderism. The second type of sinful behavior is clearly defined as homosexuality.

Unnatural Interpretations of Romans 1

The most difficult passage for gay revisionists is Romans 1:26–27:

> God gave them over to shameful lusts. Even their women exchanged natural sexual relations for unnatural ones. In the same way the men also abandoned natural relations with women and were inflamed with lust for one another. Men committed shameful acts with other men, and received in themselves the due penalty for their error.

God is an excellent communicator, and this passage is clear. Homosexuality is "unnatural" and "shameful" because it goes against God's design and damages people's souls. God loves us enough to warn us. However, gay revisionists claim that this passage explains that it's "unnatural" and sinful for heterosexuals to have same-gender sex, but natural and God-approved for homosexuals!

When revisionists claim this, they replace design with desires because they've come to see their homosexual feelings as "natural." But Scripture clearly teaches that feelings and desires are never a reliable basis to determine right and wrong. In fact, Christians are commanded "to put off" our old self, "which is being corrupted by its deceitful desires" (Eph. 4:22).

Romans is talking about the natural design and wholesome desires God gave mankind in creation (Gen. 2:18–23). LGBTQ+ relationships are unnatural because a man is not a "suitable helper" for a man. Nor is a woman a "suitable helper" for a woman. The union of two men or two women denies God's natural design and involves methods of intercourse that aren't natural to the human body and lack the natural ability to produce children.

God's eternal, unchanging Word always, without exception, mentions homosexuality in strongly negative terms, and nothing in Romans 1:26–27 suggests God thinks it's natural for some people to have gay sex and unnatural for others.

> ***Some children may have a strong temptation to steal. But they aren't born thieves. The same is true for homosexuality.***

Nor can men or women claim they were born homosexual. After the fall of the human race, each of us was born with a natural desire to sin, and our temptations vary. Some children may have a strong temptation to steal. Or they may gain this temptation because people and influences in their lives make stealing sound good and even "natural." But they aren't born thieves.

The same is true for homosexuality. At times, homosexual desires are formed through abuse, and this is especially heartbreaking. These people need to experience the healing and restoration that only our Lord can give. And this is true for any sinful desire, no matter how it originally took hold in our lives. God wants to provide healing and restoration.

> When tempted, no one should say, "God is tempting me." For God cannot be tempted by evil, nor does he tempt anyone; but each person is tempted when they are dragged away by their own evil desire and enticed. Then, after desire has conceived, it gives birth to sin; and sin, when it is full-grown, gives birth to death. (James 1:13–15)

Basing what's natural on feelings leads to further contradictions in gay revisionist theology because most gay revisionists accept bisexuality as well as homosexuality. If gay revisionists approve bisexual desires as natural, i.e. a person having both heterosexual and homosexual desires, then the only people Romans 1 would condemn (according to them) are those who have homosexual relationships when they have no desire to have them.

Other than victims, I'd say that group is non-existent. Yet gay revisionists believe this group is so important that God highlighted them in this strong passage about moral decline.

Basing what's "natural" upon sexual desires and attractions would require us to accept every sexual practice, including pedophilia, rape, and bestiality. And if you want to depend on human wisdom, you can even find "scientific" studies to affirm that some people are born to have sex with children and some men are born to have multiple sex partners. But like these gay revisionist arguments, these studies treat sinful desires as natural and inalterable.

This gay revisionist argument is a poor attempt to contradict the obvious message in Romans 1. And perhaps they realize this, because after making the natural/unnatural argument, some of the most prominent gay revisionists offer a second explanation that contradicts the first.

Comparing Apples and Rocks

The other revisionist explanation for this passage is even more untenable than the first. Sometimes we explain that false teachers mislead people by comparing apples with oranges. But this gay revisionist explanation of Romans 1 is more like comparing apples and rocks.

In this argument, revisionists claim that we should compare Romans 1 with First Corinthians 11, which talks about hair length and head coverings, because they both use the Greek word *phusis* to call a practice unnatural or against nature. And they both use the Greek word *atimia* meaning disgraceful or dishonorable. Therefore, gay revisionists claim that both passages discuss cultural practices, not sinful behavior.

> Because of this, God gave them over to shameful [*atimia*] lusts. Even their women exchanged natural sexual relations for unnatural [*phusis*] ones. In the same way the men also abandoned natural [*phusikos*] relations with women and were inflamed with

> lust for one another. Men committed shameful [*aschémosuné*] acts with other men, and received in themselves the due penalty for their error. (Rom. 1:26–27)
>
> Judge for yourselves: Is it proper for a woman to pray to God with her head uncovered? Does not the very nature [*phusis*] of things teach you that if a man has long hair, it is a disgrace [*atimia*] to him? (1 Cor. 11:13–14)

Words are affected by their context. For example, we can be ashamed for forgetting to return a phone call or ashamed for committing a murder. It can feel unnatural to have a heart attack or unnatural to skip breakfast. Just because the same word is used in two different passages doesn't mean the content of those passages is similar. Saying a man's long hair is culturally unnatural is very different from saying he has given himself over to a shameful, unnatural sexual lifestyle.

In First Corinthians 11, Paul discussed the cultural attitudes toward head coverings and hair length, cultural attitudes that change over time. Throughout the passage he uses words to make this clear. Paul introduces the passage as "holding to the traditions" (11:2). He calls head coverings a "practice" (11:16). He uses "conditional" wording: "If it is a disgrace for a woman to have her hair cut off or her head shaved, then she should cover her head" (11:6). "Judge for yourselves: Is it proper for a woman to pray to God with her head uncovered?" (11:13).

So let's judge for ourselves. When Paul wrote these verses, women who did not cover their heads were considered immoral, rebellious, or disrespectful. And long hair on men was seen as culturally inappropriate. Paul was telling Christians to behave in ways that represent the gospel in their specific culture and time in history.

How about today? Are women without head coverings viewed by culture and other Christians as ungodly? No. In fact, head coverings today are typically associated with the false religion of Islam. A few Christian denominations promote head coverings for women, but this passage is not a moral command.

Regarding men's hair length, in our culture it depends more on styling than on length. Long hair can make a man look gay or effeminate, but that is not necessarily true.

If we doubt that this is a cultural command, we can look at the Old Testament command for Nazirite men in Numbers 6:1–21. Numbers 6:5 says, "During the entire period of their Nazirite vow, no razor may be used on their head. They must be holy until the period of their dedication to the LORD is over; they must let their hair grow long."

Long hair on men was considered unnatural and disgraceful in First Corinthians 11:14, but it was considered holy in Numbers 6:5. This proves that we are dealing with a cultural situation, not one related to creation design.

Every mention of homosexuality in the Old and New Testaments is negative. Paul wasn't simply defining a cultural view. He was expressing a moral standard.

Unlike First Corinthians 11, Romans 1 doesn't contain a single word that reflects a cultural theme. It's true that both passages use the same Greek words for shameful and unnatural, but that's where the similarity ends. First Corinthians warns us that our outward appearance should reflect godliness according to cultural practices. Romans 1 talks about sins that always have been and always will be destructive to people and cultures.

Can we find another passage in Scripture where God approved homosexual behavior as He does long hair on men? No. Every mention of homosexuality in the Old and New Testaments is negative. And if that's not enough, when Romans 1 was written, Greek and Roman cultures approved of homosexual behavior in certain circumstances, so Paul wasn't simply defining a cultural view. He was expressing a moral standard.

Cultural commands are rare in the New Testament, but First Corinthians 11 is one of them, and Romans 1 is not.

Half-Truth Teaching About Sodom and Gomorrah

Another example of gay revisionists' theology is their view of Sodom and Gomorrah, claiming its destruction wasn't related to homosexuality. They base this claim on Ezekiel 16:49–50, which says the people of Sodom and Gomorrah were "arrogant, overfed and unconcerned; they did not help the poor and needy. They were haughty and did detestable things before me."

Homosexuality is not specifically mentioned in that passage and other sins were involved in Sodom and Gomorrah's evil lifestyles. But "detestable things" most certainly refers to homosexuality because "all the men from every part of the city of Sodom—both young and old—surrounded [Lot's] house. They called to Lot, 'Where are the men who came to you tonight? Bring them out to us so that we can have sex with them'" (Gen. 19:4–5).

Because this attempt at homosexual gang rape was a key element in the destruction of these cities, gay revisionists insist that the rape was condemned, not the homosexual lifestyle. However, they still have to deal with Leviticus 20:13 and 18:22–24, Romans 1:26–32, First Corinthians 6:9–11, and First Timothy 1:8–11—which all condemn homosexual behavior in general.

But the most obvious verse to refute this claim about the sins of Sodom and Gomorrah is Jude 1:7: "Sodom and Gomorrah and the surrounding towns gave themselves up to sexual immorality and perversion. They serve as an example of those who suffer the punishment of eternal fire."

The Greek word translated "sexual immorality" includes any immoral sexual practice, and the one translated "perversion" refers to unnatural sexual practices, such as homosexuality. It's more literally translated (in the KJV) as "going after strange flesh."

Does God Hate Shrimp?

A popular question gay revisionists ask is, "Does God hate shrimp?" The Old Testament forbids both homosexuality and eating shrimp. Since New Testament teachings say nothing about eating shrimp, revisionists claim Old Testament laws against homosexuality are also no longer pertinent.

This argument breaks down quickly when we realize that Jesus ended Old Testament dietary laws in Mark 7:18–19, and this truth was further emphasized in Acts 10. We don't fully understand why God considered certain foods "unclean" during Old Testament times. Possibly some were unsafe or unhealthy due to ancient methods of cleaning and storing food.

But the Old Testament dietary, cleansing, and ceremonial laws had multiple purposes. For one thing, they proved that external law-keeping doesn't change hearts or make people right with God, thus preparing us for the coming of Christ (Rom. 3:19–20; 4:13–14; Gal. 3:23–25). Christ didn't abolish these laws, but He fulfilled them, meaning we are no longer required to obey them (Matt. 5:17).

Besides dietary, cleansing, and ceremonial laws, civil laws were given to Israel for a specific time in history. Some of these laws reflect biblical principles, but they are not permanent commands. For instance, as we explained in Chapter 14, Leviticus 20:13 commands that homosexuals be put to death. The New Testament condemns homosexuality, but it does not call for homosexuals to be executed.

But the main way to put this revisionist claim to rest is to ask if the law is part of the New Covenant—the New Testament commands. Homosexuality is clearly condemned in the New Testament, but eating shrimp is not.

Confused Views of Acts 10

Another purpose of God's Old Testament dietary laws was to set Israel apart from the pagan nations around them, building their faith and calling them to purity. God did this so they could eventually be a blessing to the Gentile nations (Gen. 12:1–3; 18:18; Gal. 3:14).

When Christ died, He fulfilled the law, and we came under grace (Matt. 5:17; Rom. 6:14). Instead of the ceremonial, sacrificial, dietary, and cleansing laws, we came under the law of Christ, which means we obey His commands because we love Him (1 Cor. 9:19–23; 1 John 2:3).

But Peter and many Jewish Christians had trouble giving up these external Old Testament laws. After all, the laws were part of their Jewish upbringing. So in Acts 10, God helped Peter fully understand that the Old Covenant rules had ended so that Peter would be prepared to share Christ with Gentiles, specifically with Cornelius.

Gay revisionists claim that Acts 10 was not only God's way of showing the Jews to accept the Gentiles, but they claim it was also God's way of showing the Jews to accept sexual lifestyles previously condemned. When I studied this revisionist claim, I was surprised to find that it has been used for more than fifty years by homosexuals seeking to justify their behavior.[2]

Comparing ethnicity to sexual lifestyles is a popular way to discredit Christians as "racist," but it's not accurate or logical. Ethnicity is determined by God, who places us in a specific family, race, country, and time in history (Acts 17:24–28). Homosexuality is a human behavioral choice that contradicts God's design and purposes for mankind (Rom. 1:24–27). There's no comparison.

---

2 For example, see Walter Brueggemann, "How to read the Bible on homosexuality," *Outreach: An LGBTQ Catholic Resource*, September 4, 2022 (https://outreach.faith/2022/09/walter-brueggemann-how-to-read-the-bible-on-homosexuality/).

Secondly, Acts 10 confirms that Gentiles should be told about salvation. It doesn't confirm they are righteous or saved.

Those who want to emphasize homosexuality when reading Acts 10 could say this passage makes it clear that Gentile homosexuals can be saved in the same way Jewish homosexuals can be saved: by repenting and turning to Christ so He can set them free from their sins, including the sin of homosexuality (Acts 3:19; 1 Cor. 6:9–11).

The reason Christians have called homosexuality a sin throughout history is because the Bible clearly teaches that it *is* a sin.

We Christians are responsible to share what the Bible teaches about sexual sin and offer a message of hope that sets homosexuals and other sinners free from sins that damage their hearts, souls, and bodies.

Teachings That Bear Bad Fruit

Matthew 7:15–18 is another passage revisionists use to claim that the Bible doesn't teach against homosexual behavior.

> Watch out for false prophets. They come to you in sheep's clothing, but inwardly they are ferocious wolves. By their fruit you will recognize them. Do people pick grapes from thornbushes, or figs from thistles? Likewise, every good tree bears good fruit, but a bad tree bears bad fruit. A good tree cannot bear bad fruit, and a bad tree cannot bear good fruit.

You might wonder how this passage could be used to support homosexual behavior, but it shows the innovative nature of false teachings. Revisionists claim that if a biblical teaching is good, it won't make anyone feel ashamed. Therefore, since teachings against homosexuality offend homosexuals, make them feel judged, and prevent them from same-sex relationships, those teachings can't be "good fruit."

But that has nothing to do with the message of this passage. It's talking about the fruit of godliness, purity, and peace we enjoy when we are living as God designed. When we are disobedient, God's commands should make us feel bad.

Making men and women ashamed of their sins is a "good fruit" because it leads them to repent and receive the forgiveness of God. Jesus said, "Those whom I love I rebuke and discipline. So be earnest and repent" (Rev. 3:19).

Revisionists are again basing their beliefs on feelings and desires instead of God's truth. James 4:8–10 tells us that we should feel terrible about our sins: "Come near to God and he will come near to you. Wash your hands, you sinners, and purify your hearts, you double-minded. Grieve, mourn and wail. Change your laughter to mourning and your joy to gloom. Humble yourselves before the Lord, and he will lift you up."

Arguments Used to Affirm Transgenderism

We addressed transgenderism in Chapter 14, but let's look at some of the arguments used to defend it. Some people claim that extensive research, interviews, and surveys prove that some people are born another gender than their body type.

Many studies presented as scientific are strongly influenced by culture and worldview.

Regarding research studies, we can probably find a study to support or refute just about any view we hold. Many studies presented as scientific are strongly influenced by culture and worldview.

One of the most famous studies on human sexuality is the Kinsey Report. Kinsey used unscientific methods and reached biased conclusions because much of his study focused on aberrant behavior, based on interviews with prostitutes, homosexuals, and pedophiles. Yet his study continues to be cited as authoritative.[3]

Kinsey's study subtly implied that all forms of sexual behavior should be considered valid. But Christians base our views on God's Word, not on research studies.

Another claim of transgender proponents is that children instinctively know they are another sex, even when no adult has influenced them. That claim is irrational since children often believe they're animals, princesses, and superheroes. Children also believe in Santa Claus and the tooth fairy. They love fantasy and have trouble at times distinguishing it from reality.

Because they don't have mature logic and reasoning skills, we don't allow children to decide their bedtime or their diet. Allowing them to make a "decision" about their gender is nothing less than child abuse. Good parents guide and direct their children according to God's Word. They don't let their children guide and direct them.

Another claim used to support transgenderism is that some animals can change gender (e.g., clownfish), proving it's a healthy part of God's design. But Scripture explains that humans are created in the image of God and set apart from animals (Gen. 1:26–28).

Some male animals chase female animals when they're fertile, impregnate them, and leave, taking no responsibility for the baby animals. If animals justify human behavior, we could conclude that God designed some men to rape women and abandon them. We could make countless ridiculous comparisons if we use animal design and behavior to justify human design and behavior.

---

3 *Newsweek*, "Weird Science: Kinsey's Pedophile," March 13, 2010 (https://www.newsweek.com/weird-science-kinseys-pedophile-180414); Rockefeller Archive Center, "Funding a Sexual Revolution: The Kinsey Reports," January 9, 2020 (https://resource.rockarch.org/story/funding-a-sexual-revolution-the-kinsey-reports/).

As Christians, we know that God not only created us uniquely higher than animals, He also created our sexual identity from the moment of conception.

In extremely rare cases, babies are born with atypical genitalia. These children are sometimes mentioned to support transgenderism, but this is a birth defect, and gender is often resolved with DNA tests. Using these children to justify transgenderism is like using children born blind to justify a child poking out his eyes.

The Clarity and Consistency of God's Word

God's Word is not a puzzle that says one thing but means another. Some mystery is involved in our relationship with God because we are finite beings seeking to understand an infinite God (1 Cor. 13:12). But God's Word gives us all the clarity we need to understand His earthly purposes for us, and He has given us clear commands about our sexual behavior.

> His divine power has given us everything we need for a godly life through our knowledge of him who called us by his own glory and goodness. (2 Pet. 1:3)

Satan loves revisionist "theologies" because they keep people from inheriting the kingdom of God. He knows that when homosexuals repent and turn to Jesus, they'll be freed from harmful lifestyles, finding forgiveness and inheriting eternal life.

These revisionist teachings can be highly deceptive (2 Tim. 4:3; Jude 1:18). So, let's study God's Word and heed this warning: "See to it that no one takes you captive through hollow and deceptive philosophy, which depends on human tradition and the elemental spiritual forces of this world rather than on Christ" (Col. 2:8).

Digging Deeper: Questions for Group or Personal Study

1. Besides those reasons mentioned in this chapter, what other reasons make it ironic for gay revisionists to use Matthew 7:15–18 to support their false teachings?

2. The transgender claims about animal behavior deny basic truths in Genesis 1:26–28, Psalm 8:4–8, Matthew 10:29–31, 6:26, and 12:11–12. How do these Scriptures also apply to those who consider animal rights equal to human rights?

3. How does First John 2:18–19 help us understand why many churches and "Christian" leaders are now affirming immoral lifestyles?

4. Some Christians are deceived by these revisionist claims. Consider ways you can make yourself familiar with these false arguments so you can address them biblically and graciously when someone brings them up.

Conclusion

The Whole Truth

WHEN PAUL SAID goodbye to the Ephesians in Acts 20, he knew he was facing greater persecution and hardship, and he would never see the Ephesians again. He explained some important elements of maintaining true faith:

> You know that I have not hesitated to preach anything that would be helpful to you but have taught you publicly and from house to house. I have declared to both Jews and Greeks that they must turn to God in repentance and have faith in our Lord Jesus. . . . my only aim is to finish the race and complete the task the Lord Jesus has given me—the task of testifying to the good news of God's grace. . . . I am innocent of the blood of any of you. For I have not hesitated to proclaim to you the whole will of God. . . . after I leave, savage wolves will come in among you and will not spare the flock. Even from your own number men will arise and distort the truth in order to draw away disciples after them. So be on your guard! Remember that for three years I never stopped warning each of you night and day with tears.
>
> Now I commit you to God and to the word of his grace, which can build you up and give you an inheritance among all those who are sanctified. (Acts 20:20–32)

Paul had proclaimed the whole will of God, the full counsel, the complete plan and purpose of God. He warned the Ephesians that people would distort the things he'd taught them. In fact, there would be some people inside their own fellowship who would do so.

This warning was true in Paul's day and it's true in ours. The only way we can avoid half-truth teachings is by carefully studying what Scripture actually teaches.

As we've discussed in previous chapters, knowing the full will of God requires putting things in context. Phrases must be put in the context of the sentence, paragraph, section, and chapter. And most importantly, all things must be put in the context of the full teaching of God's Word.

The Studied Truth

> Do your best to present yourself to God as one approved, a worker who does not need to be ashamed and who correctly handles the word of truth. (2 Tim. 2:15)

We cannot grow in our faith unless we study God's Word carefully, regularly, and deliberately. We're meant to be lifelong students in this regard, continually increasing our knowledge and appreciation for Scripture and applying it to our lives.

This means understanding the purpose of books such as Proverbs, realizing it's not a book of promises. It means understanding the unfolding revelation in God's Word, realizing the difference between Old Testament laws and promises and New Testament commands and promises. It means fully trusting the miracles in Scripture while discerning figurative language.

The Detailed Truth

> We demolish arguments and every pretension that sets itself up against the knowledge of God, and we take captive every thought to make it obedient to Christ. (2 Cor. 10:5)

There is no such thing as a small error when it comes to God's Word. In fact, as we've seen throughout the chapters of this book, the "small" errors are what typically lead to enormous misunderstandings. We wouldn't eat a cookie if the baker replaced a teaspoon of salt with a teaspoon of poison, but we often accept teachings that replace a "teaspoon" of truth with a "teaspoon" of lies that are every bit as damaging as poison.

Matthew 7:15 and Second Corinthians 11:13–15 explain that false teachings are usually presented attractively. This is especially true in regard to some popular "Christian" novels, miniseries, movies, and seminars.

Sadly, these attractive presentations cause undiscerning Christians to believe half-truths about the gospel. And some mature Christians decide to overlook the "small" errors as long as something makes the gospel popular.

Our first loyalty must be to God's Word, accurately presented in every detail. We must be like the Bereans mentioned in Acts 17:11—people who tested everything they heard.

It's worth repeating: There is no such thing as a small error when it comes to God's Word. Guided by God's Spirit, let's study and defend the whole truth down to the smallest detail.

Digging Deeper: Questions for Group or Personal Study

1. A popular "Christian" movement claims Christmas is a pagan holiday. When I researched their claims historically, I found that they exaggerated the similarities and ignored the differences between these pagan holidays and Christmas. This was also evident in their scriptural claim that Jeremiah 10:2–4 condemns Christmas trees. Study this passage, put it in context, and list some ways it might resemble Christmas trees and ways it does not.

2. At first glance, verses 4 and 5 in Proverbs 26 appear to contradict each other. How do Colossians 4:6, Second Timothy

2:23–24, and Titus 3:10 help you better understand these two verses in Proverbs?

3. A well-known boundaries teaching claims that Matthew 18:15–20 directs us to cut off friends and family members who don't live up to our standards. How does the context of this passage refute such a claim? How do Romans 12 and Proverbs 18:1 address this claim?

4. Second Chronicles 7:14 is a popular verse. Can you explain what application it has to us at this point in history and how that differs from its application when given to the nation of Israel? Does it promise a healed land to us today? Consider the fervent prayers of those who suffer in persecuted countries. You might also gain some insights from First Timothy 2:1–4.

5. What subjects in this book had the most impact on you? Which were the most helpful? Are there teachings in the book you are having difficulty accepting?

6. There are several "Christian" movements that claim Matthew 5:17–20 requires Christians to obey Old Testament laws. They aren't consistent because they adhere to dietary and ceremonial laws, not sacrificial or cleansing laws. However, they've gathered significant followings with half-truth principles. How do these passages refute their beliefs: Galatians 2:19–21; 3:2–3; 3:12–13; Colossians 2:16–17?

7. When Paul said, "I am innocent of the blood of any of you. For I have not hesitated to proclaim to you the whole will of God" (Acts 20:26–27), he made an important statement we all must heed. See Ezekiel 33:7–9 for a fuller understanding of Paul's statement.

CLC

PUBLICATIONS

Fort Washington, PA 19034

This book is published by CLC Publications, an outreach of CLC Ministries International. The purpose of CLC is to make evangelical Christian literature available to all nations so that people may come to faith and maturity in the Lord Jesus Christ. We hope this book has been life changing and has enriched your walk with God through the work of the Holy Spirit. If you would like to know more about CLC, we invite you to visit our website:

www.clcusa.org

To know more about the remarkable story of the founding of CLC International we encourage you to read

LEAP OF FAITH

Norman Grubb

Paperback

Size $5^{1}/_{4}$ x 8, Pages 248

ISBN: 978-0-87508-650-7

ISBN (*e-book*): 978-1-61958-055-8

ESSENTIAL CHRISTIANITY

A Handbook of Basic Christian Doctrines

Dr. Walter Martin

Published originally in the 1970s, *Essential Christianity* is a readable explanation of the most important Christian teachings, with answers to such vital questions as:

IS THE BIBLE COMPLETELY TRUE?

HOW CAN GOD BE THREE IN ONE?

IS CHRIST REALLY GOD AND MAN?

WHO WILL BE SAVED IN THE END?

... plus dozens more crucially important questions about God, man and the universe. *Essential Christianity* will give you the answers you need in our confusing world of cults, half-truths, and religious confusion.

Paperback
Size 5 1/4 x 8, Pages 144
ISBN: 978-1-61958-344-3
ISBN (*e-book*): 978-1-61958-345-0